GW00726804

REAL stuff:

A SURVIVOR'S GUIDE

HEATHER JAMISON
with BRIAN JAMISON & HENRY J. ROGERS

REAL stuff:

A SURVIVOR'S GUIDE

Real Stuff: A Survivor's Guide
© 2006 by Heather Jamison

Published by Kregel Publications, a division of Kregel, Inc., P.O. Box 2607, Grand Rapids, MI 49501.

All rights reserved. No part of this book may be reproduced, stored in a retrieval system, or transmitted in any form or by any means—electronic, mechanical, photocopy, recording, or otherwise—without written permission of the publisher, except for brief quotations in printed reviews.

Unless otherwise indicated, Scripture quotations are from *The Message*. Copyright © 1993, 1994, 1995, 1996, 2000, 2001, 2002. Used by permission of NavPress Publishing Group. All rights reserved.

Scripture quotations marked NASB from the NEW AMERICAN STANDARD BIBLE, updated edition. Copyright © 1960, 1962, 1963, 1968, 1971, 1972, 1973, 1975, 1977, 1995 by The Lockman Foundation. Used by permission. (www.Lockman.org)

Library of Congress Cataloging-in-Publication Data
Jamison, Heather.
Real stuff : a survivor's guide / by Heather Jamison with Brian Jamison and Henry J. Rogers.
    p. cm.
    Includes bibliographical references (p.   ).
    1. Teenage girls—Religious life. 2. Teenage girls—Conduct of life. I. Jamison, Brian. II. Rogers, Henry J. III. Title.
    BV4551.3.J36 2006
    248.8'33-dc22   2006008354

ISBN 0-8254-2931-5

Printed in the United States of America

06 07 08 09 10 / 5 4 3 2 1

Brian and Heather would like to dedicate
this book to their three girls—
Bryanne, Tayte, and Katerisha.

Henry and his wife, Kathy, would like to
dedicate this book to their three girls—
Gabrielle, Whitney, and Zoya.

CONTENTS

HEY!

HEY there!

This is the "**HEY!**" part, the place where we get to meet for a bit and I tell you how the book you're holding came to be (other than the actual book-binding process which is, admittedly, interesting, but can get boring eventually). Sure, some people usually call that an "introduction" or something else like that. You can even get really fancy and call it a (drum roll, please) . . . prologue.

But not me. I'm going basic here . . . primarily because I'm selfish. I know that if I were you and I saw the big, bold letters announcing an "Introduction," well . . . I'd skip it. I'd flip through the book to the part on boys and sex, and then I'd quickly skim through that section for any new info on body parts that I hadn't yet heard about. And I'd also make up my mind in a paragraph or two if (a) the writer was a sheltered, head-in-the-clouds, never-been-tempted gal, (b) if she was just a goon from the fourteenth century, or (c) if I thought I could trust her.

Then I'd stick the book back on my shelf and tell my mom that I read it. **HEY**, I did read it . . . kind of. Okay, I'd tell her I read *some* of it. And then I'd move on to more noble and important things in my life, like painstakingly matching the color of my lipstick to the upside-down letters on my new shirt, or going shopping for the perfect pair of jeans that didn't make my rear end look too big.

So that's what I would do if confronted with the big, bad, bold letters of the "Introduction."

And that's why I've avoided this unforgivable error.

So, this, my lovely girlfriend, will just be the "**HEY**" part. Real smooth, huh? Like, **HEY**, how ya doing? How's school? The friends? The youth group? The fam? How's that new guy who totally makes your stomach go into more twists and turns than the latest roller coaster ride at the amusement park? He's cute, isn't he? And smart? (Okay, I hear ya, we'll leave it at cute. Cute's okay. Who needs brains these days, anyhow, what with technology and all.)

And yeah, sure, you'd probably rather be with him right now instead of reading this book; but, **HEY**, your mom did buy it for you, didn't she? Or *someone* did, most likely, and you are a tadpole-bit curious about the things we're going to talk about. Because the reality is, life does get hard sometimes . . . and confusing. And although you may not admit it, which is cool, sometimes you want some help, some advice. And maybe by now the subject caught your interest, which I hope it did. Because this book is for you.

For you and you alone.

That is why I wrote it.

And contrary to popular opinion, I didn't write this book for your mom to buy it, so that it could end up on your shelf—unread—underneath your outdated collection of CDs and the rough draft for your "original idea" science paper on why you think Adam had a belly button.

I wrote it to be read—really—and not just by your youth pastor . . . or your Sunday school teacher . . . or your auntie.

I wrote it for you.

I believe in the message of this book, I guess because I know the heart behind it. I still bear the scars from the lessons that were learned while preparing for it. I'd jump up and down and then do a back handspring right now if I knew you would avoid learning some of those lessons the hard way by reading this. I want you to read it.

Really. Really!

And I want you to read all of it.

I know. Tall order.

But, **HEY**, I've tried to make this book short, simple, to the point, and about things that really matter. I did that for you. There's not going to be one word on the Renaissance. I promise. And I can guarantee you that I won't ever talk about the London Fire in the seventeenth century, or the one in Chicago where the cow kicked over the bucket and started the whole flaming thing.

Nor am I even going to mention the best way to make an apple streusel (like how you really need to go easy on the brown sugar). And you won't hear me spill the beans about anything on the czar of Russia. There won't be anything on Anastasia, either. And you can just forget about ever hearing anything on the Boer battles in South Africa.

Instead, we're going to talk about the basics. The simple things in life. But I suppose sometimes the simple things are the things that end up not being all that simple, right? So, really, we're going to talk about the simple-things-that-end-up-not-being-all-that-simple.

Like rules.

Oh—yuck—not that word! (I can see you grimacing already, tempted to toss this book in with your mom's stew.) I know where you're coming from. Rules. They can be a drag sometimes. And I'm going to keep it real with you in this book, so I'll start now. I'm not a big fan of rules either. But we'll get to that later.

Moving on. We're also going to talk about rags, those wonderful, artistic clothing endeavors that we wrap around our bodies every day to make statements on style, purpose, meaning, value, and the overall temperature in our area.

And then, of course, what teen book would be complete without a section on relationships? So we're going to talk about the things that make them tick . . . or tock . . . or talk (as in the gossip rows, that is). We'll talk about the things that make them work, and the things that make them hurt.

Rules. Rags. Relationships.

That's it. Pretty simple, huh?

Yeah, you're right. Those things aren't simple at all. They're complex. Confusing. Frustrating. Freeing. Annoying. Invigorating. Crushing.

And so we're going to dig in, girls. We're going to get dirty. We're going to hear things that maybe make us a bit uncomfortable. And things that bring out some yucky feelings from our long-ago (or not-so-long-ago) past. Some of these things will make us angry. Some will make us laugh.

But, **HEY**, that's the stuff of life. The real stuff.

And by the time you're done with this book, I hope that you somehow know your heart better on these things and, more importantly, know that your heart is true. Mine is.

But it has taken me a lot longer than I expected to get there and to put the words in this book together. In fact (shhh, don't tell anyone), I'm a wee late even getting this to my publisher. They asked me if I would write it way back when the dinosaurs still roamed—around 2002. And me—being the eager beaver that I am—said, sure, **HEY**, why not?

But God had better plans.

But before I divulge the story, how about ordering us up a couple of tall mochas with whipped cream on top. Let's get cozy first because it's about to get real.

MOCHA MEMORIES

You sipping your mocha or licking the cream? Me too. I always ask for extra cream, kind of like, "Hey, make mine a tall whipped cream with a shot of mocha, please." Okay, now . . . where did I leave off? Ah yes, I said sure, but God had other plans.

He knew I still had some massive lessons that needed to be learned, some pride that needed to be burned, some understanding that needed to be got, and some grace that needed to be sought.

And accepted.

That's the hard part, isn't it? Accepting grace?

But we've got to accept it. We really do.

So, yes, I'm a little late on my deadline. A few years, that's all. Good thing this isn't sophomore English class or I would have flunked. Good thing, too, that my publisher was cool about the whole deal and gave me an extension of another year, which I managed to be late on again. Oops. And it's a good thing that they basically ended up saying, hey, Heather, when do *you* think you can get it to us?

And, hence—voilà!—another new deadline.

You see, there was a small reason behind my dragging my feet (or rather, my dragging of my computer keys) in this process. I didn't want to just jump in and crank out into the Christian book world another *7 Steps to a Happy Teen Life Even Though You're Miserable, Ugly, and Bloated!* or here's another one, *8 Ways to Keep the Weight,*

Embrace the Identity, but Still Look Like You've Got a Smaller Bottom Than Britney! or my favorite, *You've Got Zits? I've Got Zits. All God's Children Got Zits! Let's Pop Them and Party! Chips, Anyone?*

To be honest, I don't have time for meaningless talk like that, nor for meaningless answers. I don't have an interest in encouraging it, either. Some things I pick up and read are really powerful, but other things leave me wondering what planet the writer lives on.

I want to yell: No! Everything is not made all-of-a-sudden-better with a quiet time and a Bible verse taped on your mirror. Pimples don't go away because of praise songs, and hearts don't heal because of a day spent in a soup kitchen serving the poor and homeless.

I'm not dissing God's Word, or worship, or service—hey, I'm married to a man who has spent a good number of years teaching pastors in Africa! I believe in the stuff or I wouldn't be behind him. But life is too complicated to solve with a verse picked at random, an act of service, or a new song. Or even a book with a clever title but no content.

It's our heart that really matters.

It's our mind that truly makes us.

Our actions are simply the result.

To be honest, girls, we are complex, imprinted, shaped individuals. From birth, our wrong thinking and wrong attitudes about life, ourselves, others, and even God have been taking form. It's not disrespectful to say that it might take a lot to reform all that dysfunction. It might take some tears. In fact, for many of us, it most likely will. It might take letting go of some fears, fears we actually cling to for a false sense of safety and comfort. It might take a relearning of who we truly are—what drives us, defeats us, inspires us, and depletes us.

So that's why this book was a tad late to the publishers, that's why I didn't hit my deadline, or even get close. Because I was still making my own journey across the Plains of Gorgoroth like poor, burdened Frodo with his Ring of Doom. I was, and am, still learning.

But, at least, by the grace of God, I think I'm to the point now where I'm ready to share a bit of that with you—deadline or not—if you'll have me. I'm ready to go through this journey again, mentally, if it'll help you find out where you are, if it will help you at all.

You see, I'm all into everyone helping each other out because I come from the era where that wasn't always the case. It wasn't okay to admit weakness, or imperfection, or pain. Somehow, I guess, the Christian leaders at that time had the mentality that to admit weakness was to somehow belittle God, rather than simply size up humanity and be honest about how imperfect we all are.

I entered adolescence before the trendy Christian teenage movements existed. Yes, I know, I'm dating myself here and revealing my age. Scary! But, really, it's okay. I'll always be younger than J-Lo and Cameron Diaz, and about the same as Jennifer Garner. And they haven't yet given in to urges of crocheting or needlework. (Nor does the impulse strike me.) So, yes, even though I'm old (at least older than you), my rocker is still stored in the attic, unused.

Now my teen years—as I was saying before you nastily pulled me away to remind me of my age—were pre-*True Love Waits,* pre-*See You at the Pole,* and pre-*Passion.* In fact, I was pretty much "premovement." There was little or no movement at all, other than, of course, the movement of teens at parties on the weekends. At which, no doubt, you could find me involved.

Hey, when I was a teen, no one had yet kissed dating good-bye. In fact, no one had said good-bye to self-gratification, shallow self-expression, and selling out. There were no prayer meetings at my high school. There weren't even any virgins on my pom-pom squad, except for me and one other girl—for a while at least.

My teen generation hadn't yet heard about HIV and how it can go heterosexual. We didn't talk about abortion, and abstinence was very hush-hush back then. Like not even a vocabulary word in English class. There wasn't a lot of good spiritual buzz going on. It was all very incognito. Christians prayed in public by pretending to scratch their eyebrows.

You know what? I regret it. Totally. I regret not having a youth pastor who spoke openly about teen issues. I regret not having any Christian artists as role models to look up to like Point of Grace, Nicole C. Mullen, and Stacy O. I regret feeling like there was no other option—that there wasn't much else I could expect in life. Clawing each other at a Friday night party, while watching *Halloween 3* and *The Texas Chainsaw Massacre* with people slicing-and-dicing each other for the twenty-first time was what teenagers did. That was just . . . normal . . . even for those of us who went to church on Sunday.

So in many ways, I am jealous of you.

I am jealous of how much is out there to encourage you to value yourself as you are valued by God, to stand up for who you are, and to save some dignity and hope for your present and future. I am happy—and jealous—that the teen-pregnancy rate in America has decreased nearly 30 percent from when I was a teenager just over a decade ago.[1] I wish someone would have told me what I am now telling you: that you are worth it. You are worth waiting for. You are worth it. You really are.

And that's why I'm going to keep telling you that over and over and over again. I hope you get sick of me saying it, because maybe then you'll have heard. Really heard. So just in case you haven't heard it yet from your friends, or youth pastor, or mentor, or your folks, or from Christian movies, or Christian music, or Christian books, or just in case you have heard it but you don't quite believe it, I'm going to keep saying it. Because it's true.

You are worth it!

Believe it.

Don't throw yourself away.

Walk with me through these plains. Let's talk a bit about rules and why we hate them. Let's chat some about the rags we wrap around our searching souls. And let's learn some from our past relationships so we can learn what we deserve now, and in the future.

We need to walk together to do this.

You know, when it comes to exercise, I like to walk alone. I like to blast my mini-iPod and even dance some, who cares if anyone is watching? But when it comes to life and experiencing it, I like to walk with someone else. With a friend. Or with my hubby, B.

Now, let me explain. "B" stands for a lot of things, actually. Brave. Brilliant. Beaut. But it also stands for Brian, which is his name, too. And, if you don't mind, I've asked B to take this walk with us as well. For the most part, he's going to chill with us, but from time to time he'll jump in and give us a guy's perspective on things, to give us the 411 on what the boys think.

B knows about that sort of stuff. He's all guy, trust me. He's also done the guy things, too. You know, football team—offensive player of the year. Baseball team—record holder. Fraternity house member. College sports scholarship. Saxophone player. And just all-around good guy. In fact, he was named Peer Counselor for the whole city-wide area when he was in high school.

But before you go thinking that B's all perfect, slow down. He'd be the first to admit that he's far from that. B's blown it, too, like most of us have. So I think you'll take to his scoop on things, since it's true.

I've also asked a guy named Henry—whom I sometimes call Uncle H—to join us as well. Now, no disrespect intended, but Uncle H has picked up some years. He might disagree, but I think that's a good thing. That's one of the reasons why I wanted him walking too . . . for his cardiovascular benefit and all. No, really, Uncle H has been around long enough to give us some insights into the mind of a guy from across the generations. Some things don't change, girls. And Uncle H will say it like it is. He's not shy. He wrote a book not too long ago challenging men to lay off the sin of porn. He speaks to teens, adults, men, and women all the time, at churches, on the radio. Wherever. He's also a chaplain—for his "real" job—at a majorly big company in a majorly big building. And, to top it off, Uncle H has a very sweet wife, Kathy, and a gaggle of teenagers of his own. Last I counted, he had four in the teen years all at once! **Whoa!**

I've asked these guys to join us from time to time on our walk. I hope you don't mind. I not only want them to give us a uniquely "guy" perspective on certain things, but sometimes I want them to chime in for an "on the other hand" look at what we're chatting about. The more the merrier, I always say. Diversity adds color to an otherwise one-dimensional portrait. And with a few of us together, things are stronger, tighter. More secure. Like a chord of three strands which is not easily broken (Eccl. 4:12).

So what do you say? Enough mocha memories about me.

Shall we press on?

Let's GO, **GIRLS!**

PART 1

RULES

CHAPTER 1

WHAT'S THE DEAL WITH THEM?

I was fifteen.

A sophomore.

And trying out for the twelve-member, high school pom-pom dance team.

It was a coveted role, although I had never actually coveted it myself. With no background in dance, I hadn't even planned on trying out for the prize. But my neighbor needed a partner since auditions were done in pairs. And she—I'm not exaggerating—pleaded with me to join her.

She promised to choreograph our short, two-minute audition. And she promised not to get upset if I stepped on her toes, or, more likely, fell down during our turn.

So I agreed.

After all, this was her big shot, her one chance at glory, her solitary opportunity to rise out of the invisible ranks of mediocrity and walk among the—can you hear the orchestra sounds building—Golden Girls.

Yes, that's what they were called, The Kearney Golden Girls.

Maybe the name was chosen because of the glitzy-gold material that made up their dazzling costumes. Or maybe it was because of the golden sparkle in the eyes of each and every member.

I don't know.

All I do know is that every girl huddling in the band room, waiting to hear the names called out for the new dance squad, wanted to be one. And, I admit, after practicing, learning the routines, and actually having a real blast when performing for the tryouts, I wanted to be one too.

But only two sophomores would be chosen.

And yet, funny enough, one would be me.

Me! No joke! I would be one of only two sophomores to make the dance team. Oh, yes, I think I've already mentioned that. But that was the big deal. That was what made it so special. Girls were startled when my name was called. Teens fainted. Sirens rang. Mothers cuddled frightened children. A bulletin was issued in the local paper.

Okay, so it wasn't really that dramatic.

But people were still surprised, especially my neighbor who was trained in dance and who, weirdly enough, didn't get chosen.

After all, I was the quiet one. I didn't pop in on too many parties my freshman year. In fact, I think the final count came to . . . um, none. I had my fill of tongue-twisting contests and saliva-exchange-adventures in junior high. I no longer saw the value in them, or in seeing how many boyfriends a girl could capture in one year, kiss, and then dump before he dumped you. The whole scene started to seem a bit silly, and a bit—I don't know—risky, as far as germs were concerned.

So I stayed clear my freshman year.

And this was my plan for my sophomore year, too, when this whole Golden Girl thing came about. Then, all of a sudden, I had these long-lost best friends morphing out of the mirrors in the bathrooms. They were meeting me before school. Friends that, for some reason or another, couldn't manage to remember my name just the year before, now amazingly not only knew my name, but they also knew where my locker was and just what party I needed to attend.

Don't worry. I didn't fall for it.

I did, however, fall for him.

Nick. Ah, Nick.

And, yes, Nick put Rick Springfield to shame. (You haven't heard of Rick Springfield?) Okay . . . let's say then, rather, Nick put that cute guy staring at you from the poster on your wall to shame, and you didn't even think that was possible! But he did.

Nick was, after all, the quarterback of our all-conference football team. He was a senior. He was not a flirt. He'd had only one girl-friend, or maybe two, before me.

He was considered off-limits to most. Too good to be had. Adored by all.

I never even thought he knew my name. But he did. He had asked for it from a friend of mine when he saw me practicing one of our oh-so-extraordinary Golden Girls routines. The friend filled him in and gave me a really good rap. So, soon enough, I was Nick's girl for football season.

Then we moved.

Yep, my folks uprooted us and we moved away.

Just after Christmas break.

New school. No Nick. No more Golden days.

No, my heart wasn't broken. Nick and I had called things off a few weeks before I left, after football season had ended. It was mutual. There was never anything there. He had been nice. Respectful.

But Nick had noticed, one too many times, that most of our conversations usually ended up with me asking him about his good friend, the one who had told him my name. And he had also noticed that when we would double out for some food with that good friend and his date, that it was usually the good friend and I who ended up talking together all night long. And laughing.

Okay, insiders, the good friend's name was Brian . . . also known as B.

Now you know.

But when I moved away, B and I were only friends too. He'd never joined the dating scene, claiming that goals, dreams, and athletics called him first.

So I went to my new town a single. But, thanks to Nick, I went with the reputation as the girl who had dated him. And for some reason, since the towns were football rivals and pretty close to each other, that meant something. Actually, it meant a lot. It gave me immediate acceptance at my new—and much larger—school. And, I'm guessing, it was the reason behind my immediate proposal as well.

First day of school.

Still a sophomore.

Second term.

The intercom scratched its ugly throat as a secretary came on with an announcement. This announcement, she told us, is from one of the esteemed students. He was popular (very), good looking (depending on your taste), athletic (no doubt), rich (cha-ching).

And he had an announcement.

"I would like to welcome Heather to our school. This being her first day, I want to make her feel welcome by inviting her to go on a date with me this weekend. As an expression of my affections, here is a rose."

No, I had never heard a high school guy talk like that either. But he did.

And just then someone approached me with a rose on this Romeo's behalf.

I smiled—giggled, actually. That's what girls do.

I was flattered.

This was a great in. All I had to do was accept this guy's offer and I'd have an immediate circle of friends. It was my first day in a big, new school, after all, and he did have a solid reputation.

It was simply too good to pass up, too easy to resist.

Then something started stirring within me. Something primordial. Primeval. Visceral. Raw.

My mouth formed the word. And out it floated.

No.

As simple as that. I said no.

I thanked him for the flower, or, rather, I thanked his humble servant for the flower. And then I politely—yet decisively—told the messenger that my answer was no.

No joke.

Really!

I've thought of that opportunity a dozen times since then. I've questioned my own survival strategies and even intelligence. That was a stupid move for the new girl on the block, very stupid indeed. And, yes, I did get dagger eyes from him for the next few months.

But, no, this guy wasn't a total jerk. He was a churchgoer and was into the new "spiritual" band U2. There was no moral reason for my refusal. Rather, it was a pure reaction out of real emotion.

I had been set up. He thought he had me.

A beautiful rose. An invite over the intercom in front of hundreds of students and even faculty.

How could I say no? Had anyone uttered that syllable to him before?

So I did.

Precisely because nobody thought that I would go against this unspoken social rule.

Rules.

Ah . . . I've hated them as long as I can remember. I'm the biggest rule-breaker around. No, I tried not to get dangerous about it and usually only broke the ones within safe-enough limits. I've never gone nuts with alcohol or drugs or speeding, probably because the effects of them scare me. But if someone said, or assumed, that I needed to do something, then I often did just the opposite . . . and broke the rule.

I graduated from high school as a junior because no one had ever done it at that school before. I was awarded the recognition of "Graduating Student Who Missed the Most Days of School" at senior breakfast. I hate to admit this, especially since my own teen daughters, Bryanne and Tayte, will no doubt be reading this (Bryanne and Tayte: Mom was wrong! Mom was wrong! Stay in school!), but most of those days were skips. Sure, I'd show up for dance team practice since I made the audition-only squad at the new school too, but showing up for class was a challenge. A lot of times I'd leave just to go do a session of tanning; and since my grades were up and my behavior decent, I don't think anyone noticed.

Trust me, I know about breaking rules. I know what it feels like to be forced under a bunch of rules. For some girls, this is okay. Some don't tend to squirm at the thought of being told what to do.

> FOR EVERY ACTION, THERE IS AN EQUAL AND
> OPPOSITE REACTION. —ISAAC NEWTON

But then there are others out there, like me, who suffocate, who become afraid, and who look for ways to push the boundaries. We want to see how far we can stretch the rules until—*snap!*—it all comes back at us, and things just fall apart.

You realize that I don't have to tell you these things. I got caught very little and my rule-breaking days could just as well be forgotten. It's not anything that I'm proud of. In fact, I'm ashamed.

But there's a reason behind this madness. There's a reason lurking behind everything we do. And it seems to me that when we explore and uncover these reasons we find that it's not really the rules . . . it's not really the food . . . it's not really the clothes . . . it's not the friends that control us.

It's our nature.

That's why we do the things we do.

For many of us, rules show themselves as a threat to our own power, our own choices, and our own will. Schools tell us that we must be in the building no later than 7:45 AM, and we scream out . . . why? Our parents tell us that, even though we are fifteen, we still can't watch everything that has a PG-13 rating on it without asking them first. And we scream out . . . why? Our pastor tells us that we need to cover up our bellies and stop wearing shirts that remind him, and the rest of the men at church, of a girlie magazine. And we scream out . . . why? Our P.E. teacher says that we must climb to the ceiling using only our arms, legs, and a rope.

Why?

Our boyfriend tells us that we need to let him see us naked—all the way naked—if we love him at all. He promises not to touch.

But **Why?**

Our television tells us that we need to weigh roughly the same amount as a starving Sudanese girl in a refugee camp if we are to be considered beautiful.

Why?

Our magazines tell us that freckles should be air-brushed away and thighs photo-shopped down to the size of a walking stick.

Why?

Our God tells us that we should love one another even though Kelly keeps backstabbing and Trevor bragged to the whole team, at your expense, about his conquest on your date last week (even though it's totally untrue).

Why?

Unfortunately, though, the question of "why" rarely gets answered. Rather, we hear . . . because I told you to . . . because you're supposed to . . . because that's what good girls do . . . because that's what cool girls do . . . because that's what the Bible says somewhere . . . or just because.

So we shuck the rules.

We decide we're done with them. We're over it.

We toss them out the window and decide that we'll create our own rules—our own way of living—or at least we try to.

Why?

[HENRY TALKS]

Hey, girls. I need to put my two cents in here, because I think it's possible to get a little carried away. We can be a bit too quick to toss out the rules just because we don't always get the answer that we want when we question them. I get Heather's passion about this, but I think that what she's expressing can be confusing for some of you, and I realize that things are tough enough for you already.

Anyhow, I like rules. They make me feel safe.

Okay. Now don't check out on me just yet and skip to the next section. Grab some bottled water and an open ear and let's think this through.

Can we not all agree that rules sometimes have a purpose? Like, maybe, to protect us, to structure things? What if we didn't have stoplights and there were no rules to driving? Wasn't it you, Heather, my missionary friend in Africa, who complained to me once that there didn't seem to be any rules to driving in Kenya? It's not good, is it? People get hurt. People get killed.

And what about sports? A lot of you girls are involved in sports like soccer, basketball, or cross country. You don't deliberately try to break the rules of the game, do you? If there were no *rules* then there would be no *game*. We need time limits, and fouls, and a point system.

Rules aren't all bad.

What about the rule that says you get to leave school when the bell rings after your final class? Now that's a pretty great rule!

Rules don't always have to cramp us.

One time I was driving and missed a turn because of construction. I ended up going head-on into a huge concrete wall. My car became an accordion. Onlookers who had rushed to my aid said they didn't know how I could have survived at all! But I survived that crash because of God's grace and because of rules. Rules like driving the speed limit and wearing a seatbelt. When I lost control and headed toward that concrete barrier, I thought I was a dead man. I thought that was it for me—no more cheese pizza and fat free chocolate chip ice cream (okay, forget the fat free).

But God spared me. And He used the rules that I was obeying to do it. Had I been going 70 mph, it is doubtful that I would have made it long enough to take another breath.

But you know what? My little brother wasn't so fortunate in his car accident a few years back.

He died, largely because he wasn't following a state rule, the law that says a person shouldn't drive drunk.

I wish beyond all wishes that my brother would have followed the rules. I wish that so badly! But no matter if I wish as hard as I can on any star or planet or on anything, I can't bring him back. I so wish I could because I miss him a ton. A lot of people miss him.

People suffer when rules are broken.

I'll give you this: I know some rules are wrong, or just plain confusing. But then you must give me this: we are often protected when we follow the rules, and we often experience deep pain when we don't.

Rules have a reason.

Okay, Uncle H. I hear you, of course. Rules can keep us safe. Rules aren't all bad.

Let me just back up and say that I'm not trashing the rules entirely. I'm just noting our response to them.

I think that for many of us, our response is natural. I don't think it's so wrong to admit it. We see a sign that says, "Don't walk on the grass!" and a lot of us want to slide right over there and put a foot-print on it, you know? Our schools say that we can't wear spaghetti strap shirts, so we go and figure out a way to wear spaghetti strap jeans instead—I mean, really, that's what a lot of them have become, isn't it? We're told not to swear—so we change the swear words by a letter or two—or say it in a foreign language. We're told that we should save sex for marriage so we learn, instead, all of the other moves, while being careful to keep ourselves—technically at least—still virgins.

I don't think I'm wrong in saying that's how a lot of us are. Even Paul admitted this when he scrawled his letter out to the dudes in Rome back in Bible land. He said something about how he would not have wanted to covet unless the law had told him not to do so. He said that the rules, or the laws, woke up something strange within his sinful heart.

He writes, "Don't you remember how it was? I do, perfectly well. The law code started out as an excellent piece of work. What happened, though, was that sin found a way to pervert the command into a temptation, making a piece of 'forbidden fruit' out of it. The law code, instead of being used to guide me, was used to seduce me" (Rom. 7:8).

And you know what? I'm afraid it does the same thing in us too, girls.

I mean, hey—it's okay to admit it, if only to me. We're going to keep it real between us. I won't tell. Do you like the rules? Or do you sometimes wonder, **Why?**

CHAPTER 2

IT'S ALL ABOUT TRUST

HEATHER: So are rules really just for breaking?

BRIAN: Well, I don't think everyone likes breaking the rules.

HEATHER: True. I guess you are a good example of that.

BRIAN: Yep. I like rules . . . a lot. People like me even make 'em up when there aren't enough of them.

HEATHER: Kinda like the Pharisees?

BRIAN: Ouch.

HEATHER: Except the Pharisees just picked the rules that they liked to obey.

BRIAN: Double ouch. Okay . . . maybe they thought that in keeping most of them they could win God's approval.

HEATHER: But deep down, did they really think that was enough?

[BRIAN TALKS]

Well let's talk some background here. Back in the day, Moses had given the people God's laws. Believe me, they had enough laws. But the Pharisees—who were the religious leaders of the day—wanted more. Why? It made them feel strong and in control to make and keep rules. So they added some really crazy things, like it would be against the law to take more than a certain number of steps on a Saturday. The Pharisees got so good at making these extra rules that they began to ignore the heart behind the laws that God had given them. They began focusing on their own rules instead of God's.

And then Jesus calls them on it. He gets after them saying, "You're hopeless, you religious scholars and Pharisees! Frauds! You keep meticulous account books, tithing on every nickel and dime you get, but on the meat of God's Law, things like fairness and compassion and commitment—the absolute basics!—you carelessly take it or leave it" (Matt. 23:23).

See, they didn't just neglect the laws that mattered. They also forgot something even more important . . . humility. They got so good at keeping these silly laws that somehow made them feel more cool, more holy, and more "right" than the next guy, that they even got to the point where they didn't necessarily think that they needed God. Why did they need Him if they were doing so well on their own?

Maybe they thought that if they obeyed a lot of the rules God would be forced to grant His acceptance and approval. And, on top of that, if they were accused of anything they could point to all the rules that they kept and declare their innocence.

But I think it was even more. I think that they knew there was bad inside of them, and they were afraid of letting those things be seen, especially by God. Maybe they thought if they kept a bunch of rules God would have to say, hey, look at that one! That one is doing so well that I'm going to grant my approval and my rewards and . . . who knows what else.

Don't we do the same thing today? Well, at least some of us do. I know that I found a lot of pride in not participating in the fraternity parties, not getting drunk, and not swearing at school. It made me feel somewhat more important (pride) than everyone else. It made me feel that God had to acknowledge me as a little bit better (pride) and not quite as bad (pride) as I knew, instinctively, I was.

Joshua Harris, an author and conference speaker for teens and adults, is another guy who says, basically, the same thing about the comfort of rules. He writes in one of his books, "I guess we wanted rules. We wanted to know we were pleasing God. The whole process of becoming holy seemed complicated to us, so the idea of reducing our faith to a manageable list of promises and prohibitions was appealing."[1]

As long as I kept a good list of things that I'm doing outwardly then no one could accuse me of what I really know, that I'm a sinful person in desperate need of a Savior with no earthly idea of how to really please Him.

As long as I never watch a rated-R movie, never flip through a Sports Illustrated Swimsuit issue, never actually sit through a bad VH1 music video, never trash my parents or family with my words, never miss church or youth group, attend one mission trip a year, and serve food to the homeless on Thanksgiving, then I don't have to accept the full weight of my own sin.

Yes, Jesus did die for me. I know that. But for someone caught up in rules and their own attempt to keep them, it becomes easy to believe that maybe my part in His death was only one of the whips coming down on Him at the beginning of the process. I convince myself that everyone else contributed to the rest. It takes the guilt away, and the humility, too.

As if that's not bad enough, there's more. When I'm thinking like this then the rules begin to actually push me further away from God. By becoming more "holy" outwardly, I actually become more sinful within. I know it sounds weird, but it's true. The rules somehow begin to eclipse God's proper place in my life and in my heart. The rules, in themselves, become my new focus . . . my new god.

So, for people like me, rules can be a distraction from a true relationship with God. But I realize that isn't the case for everyone.

Got it, Brian. People like you love rules—or at least the ones that are easy to keep. But people like me are frightened by the rules.
So what do we do?

We fight them.

But why? Why do we push so much? Why do we question so much?

Let me try and explain through an image, a mental picture.

Imagine yourself standing, standing on a platform suspended five hundred feet above the roaring Nile River below. Beneath you lurk hungry crocodiles, ravenous hippos, and large boulders that could easily break your body in two, should you hit them, which you probably would if you fell.

You walk to the edge of the platform on which you are standing. Your breath becomes shallow. You study the scene. You look at your feet, remembering how faithful they have been. You see the stairs that you climbed to get there. You understand stairs. You understand platforms. You understand walking. Climbing. Going up, and going back down. This is all familiar to you. You can control it. You can stop when you want, or start again. There would be no surprises on the stairs.

But today you won't be going back down those stairs. Instead, today, a chord is fastened to the harness that hugs you tightly around your waist . . . like a child unwilling to let go. A chord that is also fastened, just as firmly, to the platform. A chord that will, ultimately, save you—because you are about to risk your everything.

You peer over the edge, looking down again. A giant hawk soars effortlessly beneath you. He reminds you that because of your limitations as a human, you could never soar like him. You would, instead, simply fall.

Yet, knowing this, you step.

Into nothing.

Into air.

And you tumble below.

The chord securely grasps you—it catches you—just moments before you are to join the hippos and the boulders and the crocodiles with their fierce jaws.

And yet the chord holds you.

Securely.

After all, you knew it would or you never would have jumped.

It's all about trust, girls.

It's all about trust.

Yes, I hear you. Sometimes it's difficult to trust the words of a youth pastor who tends to play favorites with certain girls who appear to be a bit cuter than you. And sometimes it's hard to trust that your folks really do have your best interest in mind when it looks like they have no problem throwing all your plans out the window for their job-related move. It could even be a challenge to trust your teachers when they sometimes don't seem to know the answers to your questions—on subjects that they teach.

So why do we fudge the rules? Why do we push the limits? Why do we question authority? Why do we sometimes balk in the face of familiar, yet imposing, guidelines?

We do so because, ultimately, we do not trust.

We simply do not trust.

And disobedience is always linked to a lack of trust.

Listen to the words of author John Piper in his book, *A Godward Life:* "Can you be loving and trusting and submitted to God as a *whole person,* and yet distrust his wisdom and goodness in something he says (which is what disobedience is)? If you consistently reject God's counsel in one area, can you really say that your heart is an obedient heart, even if you outwardly comply with other commandments?"[2]

It doesn't matter if we're really great at being on time for basketball practice. And it doesn't matter if we've memorized all of our Sunday school verses since the fourth grade. It doesn't matter if our bed is made and our teeth are brushed every morning. Or if we have a weekly prayer time with our classmates.

None of these things really matter nor will they protect us if our savage and selfish hearts have not yet been totally tamed and submitted to the only thing that truly is good on this earth . . . which is God.

If we follow only what we want to—what is convenient, what doesn't threaten us—we're not being obedient at all. We are simply picking and choosing our own way.

We say to ourselves, okay, I buy that rule; that rule makes sense. I'll follow that one. Like the rule about not taking a bath with the radio plugged in nearby. Because if we accidentally dropped the radio and it fell in the water we were sitting in, well we'd probably end up a little crispy with burns and electric shock. Okay, truth be told, we would die. And, on top of that, we would die with a frizz. And everybody knows that frizzes went out of style over a decade ago!

So we obey the rule about not taking a bath next to a plugged in appliance, because it makes sense.

But God is not so interested, girls, in our logic or in our fickle obedient ways. He wants our hearts. He died for our hearts. He longs for our hearts.

He wants all of us.

He doesn't get too impressed when we obey what is common sense.

He wants us to trust *Him.*

That's what true obedience is.

When we buck the rules, we're missing it. We're looking at the wrong target.

I know I do. I know I often look at the people who make the rules or the requirements and I quickly size them up. I come to the conclusion that, you know, they're not as smart as they claim. Or I decide they don't really care about me and they're not looking out for my best interests. Maybe I write off the rule because the person let me down sometime.

To be honest, people will let us down. They already have. That's not going to stop in this lifetime. I know I've been let down. I know

I've been hurt. I'm sure you have too. I know that some of you have been hurt in ways that would make someone like Captain Jack Sparrow from *Pirates of the Caribbean* blush with shame. I know that. Trust me, I do. There isn't a story you could tell me that would shock me. I've heard it, girls. I've lived it. And it's not fun.

But it's for that very reason that I'm writing to you.

I'm writing to remind you to look where you really should.

CHAPTER 3

IT'S ALL ABOUT THE RULER

Somewhere along the line, we got our eyes off of the real rule in this life . . . and off of the real Ruler, too. We replaced God with humanity. And we confused Christ with His crippled children.

But that will never do.

Never.

Because only God wholly loves us with a heart that is true.

Okay, yes. I hear you. You tell me that your boyfriend loves you with that true heart. And I'm not going to discourage you by saying that he doesn't. He probably loves you a lot. But, by the nature of his makeup—no, I'm not accusing him of wearing your eye shadow or blush—but by the nature of his physical, human makeup, DNA, even his love, at some point, will fail you. Something in him—some selfish desire, or motive, or anything really—will become more important than you. Something else will take up space in his heart.

Only God wholly loves us.

Only God has our entire best interest at heart.

It is Him that we must trust.

It is His love that sets us free to obey . . . without fear.

But how do we know that He loves us?

How can we really, really, really and truly know that He loves us?

My simple reply to you is to listen, the next time you are able, to the sound of the rooster's crow.

Yes, a rooster.

Cock-a-doodle-doo!

There you go. Now wasn't that simple? That solves everything. Just listen to the rooster.

No, seriously. Do listen to the rooster. Let me tell you why.

I used to hear it all the time.

All the time!

When I lived in Africa where cows, sheep, goats, and pretty much everything else still runs wild, I got my fill of nature's sounds, smells, and gunky stuff that got stuck underneath my shoes. Oh joy. Tell me about it. (Hint: Be careful who you fall in love with at the age of fourteen. You might end up married to him and living in Africa someday too. Just kidding, B!)

I used to hate it, though . . . the rooster's crow. It annoyed me beyond all else.

Cock-a-doodle-doo!

Cock-a-doodle-doo!

Cock-a-doodle-doo!

I would hear this night and day. And no, contrary to popular fairytale stories and children's books, the rooster does not only crow in the morning. I've heard one start as early as an hour past midnight. And then they can continue all night long.

Cock-a-doodle-doo!

I wanted to strangle the things. And then eat them . . . with a nice honey-sauce and some mashed potatoes on the side.

But I couldn't. This was Africa. There must have been a billion of them, or more. I could never eat that much. Plus, it might have been a bit counter-productive to B's attempts at missionary work with the Kenyan pastors.

So I had to bear it. I had to somehow bear their cackling call.

Until one day the thought struck me—and it struck me hard. I realized exactly what that rooster's call reminded me of. The grave call of the rooster somberly called to me over the ages of time.

It was just after Peter's denial of Jesus.

Jesus had predicted it, of course, since He's God. He told Peter that he was going to claim that he didn't know Jesus. Peter was going to abandon his best friend, Christ.

Peter was shocked. There was no way he believed this could ever happen. After all, he had just promised to stand by Christ through thick and thin, should he need to. He'd follow Him no matter what.

But Jesus knew better.

Jesus knew that the rooster would soon crow.

And crow it did.

Right after Peter's third time of denial.

Right after Peter pained his one true Lord.

It crowed.

Loudly, since they don't crow any other way.

And Peter heard it. And he cried.

But that's not the end of the story, even though that's where I always left it before. There's more. Listen up. In the book of Luke it says that immediately after the rooster crowed, Jesus turned and looked at Peter.

Jesus caught Peter's gaze.

He held it.

And then the story continues. Jesus gets beaten. Blindfolded. Questioned. Tried. And then is forced to walk the streets of the city . . . under the weight of the cross.

He walked.

That's my point.

Jesus walked after Peter's denial.

He walked in His own free will. No one forced Him—they couldn't. No one had any real power over Christ. He could have left it all at any time, but instead, He walked.

After the rooster crowed, Jesus walked.

After the betrayal of His friend, Jesus walked.

After someone who supposedly loved Him—and had pledged undying loyalty to Him—suddenly was nowhere to be found, Jesus walked.

He walked after He had caught Peter's eyes.

You see, I can't imagine what it was like for Jesus to die for sinners who didn't really know that they needed a Savior, but to die for a friend who just betrayed you?

I can even see how God's great sacrifice for a lost and confused humanity was motivated by deep, sincere pity. But to die with the crow of the rooster still echoing? To give life, love, years, and time to a disciple named Peter, only to have Peter deny you three times. I can't imagine all that, and then Jesus dying for Peter anyway. That seems a weight too heavy to bear. It's like, why bother dying for this dude? He's obviously worthless. He can't even keep his word for a few hours.

But it's not just Peter who made the rooster crow. It's all of us.

It's me . . . and it's you.

So maybe that's why hearing that rooster gave me the shivers. Maybe it sounded like a personal verdict being hammered down every time: we know who's guilty . . . and it is you!

You see, Jesus went to the cross knowing that we would all fail Him. He went to the cross knowing our messed up, weak ways. He went to the cross hearing our praises sung to Him on Sunday but seeing our betrayals and our shame the very next day.

To know all that and yet to continue the walk to the cross . . . is love. It is a love unlike any other. It is a love filled with grace, forgiveness, mercy, and power. This is a love that can be trusted.

Real love.

You don't have to earn it.

Anyhow, you never could. That's why He walked. That's precisely why He had to.

He walked with no expectation that we would ever return His love.

After all, He had just been denied. Did He expect the rest of us would be different?

But He walked on, so the next time you hear the rooster cry you can remember the loving footsteps of our Christ. The next time Satan wags his wimpy finger in your fallen face and accuses you of not deserving any grace, you just remind him that he's right . . . you are guilty. We all are. But that's not the point.

Jesus still walked. He still went.

After the rooster crowed. After.

And the next time Satan tries to convince you that there is no one on this earth who really loves you with a love that will never let you down, you tell him that he's right. But so what? Because there is Someone who does love you and He's not from this third rock from the sun. Someone loves you with a love that will never fail, and He will never leave you. Ever.

No matter how hard you push Him away.

And the next time that Satan puts it to you that you can't trust the rules set out before you, just tell him that he's right. Even rules change over time. But you can trust the One who told you to follow them. And if you do follow them, He'll be there to keep you the entire way.

He paid too high of a price for you, my friend. It wasn't just the blood, as gruesome as it was splattering across movie screens in the *Passion of the Christ.* And it wasn't just His death, as if that weren't enough. It wasn't just being beaten and humiliated and scarred for the sake of all mankind. No, the greater sacrifice came, really, in the separation Christ had from God—His Father. The whipping was bad. The crucifixion was horrific. But the real sacrifice occurred when Jesus' veins pulsed with the foul sins of this world . . . my sins and yours. When His perfect blood filled with the vulgar evils of those He was dying to save. And, because of it, the sacrifice was felt when God, the Father, was then forced to turn and look away.

God the Father left Him.

Naked.

Gasping.

Alone.

Straining against the weight of a million roosters' crows.

"Why have you abandoned me?" Jesus screamed in the moment of His worst pain.

And the answer was simple.

God abandoned Him because of Peter. And because of you. And because of me.

Christ was abandoned in the grip of our sins so that we would never have to fear being abandoned again.

You can trust Him, girls.

He wouldn't go through all of that just to leave you stranded.

His is a true love.

You can trust Him. You can take that step off of the platform of reason suspended above the river of denial. You can take that step out into the air of His arms and fall into the security of His ways. He will hold you as you tumble.

He'll never leave you. He will always defend

> YOUR GOD IS PRESENT AMONG YOU, A STRONG WARRIOR THERE TO SAVE YOU. HAPPY TO HAVE YOU BACK, HE'LL CALM YOU WITH HIS LOVE AND DELIGHT YOU WITH HIS SONGS. (ZEPHANIAH 3:17)

you. He will rescue you, if you let Him. He adores you. He even sings songs about you (read Zephaniah 3:17).

Now, be honest, Timberlake might sing good . . . but he's never singing about you. I know, it hurts to admit. But, girls, it's true. Face it.

My goodness, God even probably gets butterflies in His stomach as He watches you wake every morning, simply in the hopes that you might toss a greeting—or a smile—His way.

He loves you.

He really does.

Listen to the sound of His love. It is the sweet sound of a rooster crowing . . . the secure sound of a devoted and redeeming God.

You can trust Him. He didn't do the hard work—the sacrifice, the death, the resurrection—just to leave you hanging. No, He hung for you.

And all He wants in return . . . is you. He wants the best for you (read Jeremiah 29:11).

Sometimes knowing that helps us as we make decisions in our lives.

> I KNOW WHAT I'M DOING. I HAVE IT ALL PLANNED OUT—PLANS TO TAKE CARE OF YOU, NOT ABANDON YOU, PLANS TO GIVE YOU THE FUTURE YOU HOPE FOR. (JEREMIAH 29:11)

Listen for a sec to something this girl named Nat said. Nat, by the way, is Natalie Moe, a professional model. She knows the pressures of a world with glossy photos, skinny bodies, and demands. Natalie knows how wrong decisions can hurt her career. It's not all based on looks, you know. But there is something else that Natalie knows: her God loves her, and Jesus paid the price for her soul. Here's what Natalie recently said in a chat with me: "I have felt that tugging before to throw in all the rules. I'll never forget when I was confronted with the choice . . . Did I really want to compromise my standards or not? I could either go to parties that people invited me to that had drinking and drugs available . . . I could settle for talking like everyone else with a bad word here and there. I thought it might be cool to be accepted and be like everyone else I knew.

"God then tugged at my heart with a verse that hit me like a big hammer on my head. He said, 'Or do you not know that your body is a temple of the Holy Spirit who is in you, whom you have from God, and that you are not your own?' (1 Cor. 6:19 NASB).

"God showed me so clearly that what I did to my body, the choices I made, the things I looked at, said, and did, were like doing that to my Jesus because of the high price He paid for me . . . as if He were right there."

Nat is a super cool example of a gal who has taken the truth of God's love and allowed it to direct her heart and her life. (Check out her story in *Ignite the Fire*.)[1]

Rules don't have to make things drab and dreary, my lady. Actually it's when we stay within the guidelines of the rules—which were made to protect us—that we are most free. I know . . . sounds weird. But it's true. We are free from heartache. Regret. Shame. Loss.

CHAPTER 4

THE RULEBOOK

So if we're going to give rules a go, then what rules do we follow? What do we need to know? Well, actually, you might be surprised to find out that it's not quite as complicated or as confusing as you once thought. Because dealing with the rules becomes a whole lot easier when we keep our eyes on Christ.

And just to further simplify things . . . the rules all come down to just one.

No, that's not the rule to take the garbage out.

But, rather, it is the rule to love.

That's what we're told to do.

Jesus said, "'Love the Lord your God with all your passion and prayer and intelligence.' This is the most important, the first on any list. But there is a second to set alongside it: 'Love others as well as you love yourself'" (Matt. 22:37–39).

Basically He said that everything else is cake if we do this one thing: *love*.

If we love—with real love—then we've got it made. It's as simple as that. If all of our actions, thoughts, beliefs, hopes, and dreams stem from a heart of real love, then we're set.

But what is real love? That mushy-gushy feeling you get when Zach looks at you with his blue eyes? That pat on the back you give yourself when you donate three of your seventy-five stuffed animals stored in the attic to the Salvation Army collection truck? Letting your boyfriend feel you up because he's had it bad with his family and his stepdad, and the only time he smiles is when you let him do this one thing? Or unlocking your toy safe so that little sis can play with her favorite toy of yours and at least stay out of your hair while you have a friend over?

BUZZ! Wrong answer.

T'ain't love. Nope.

Let's get it straight from the source: "Love does no wrong to a neighbor; love therefore is the fulfillment of the law" (Rom. 13:10).

I also like B's definition of love that we try to obey as a family: "Love means doing what is best for another person even when the other person doesn't know what is best for himself."

But how can we love like that? You say you're not capable of such a perfect, patient, forgiving love. And I say, you're probably right. I know I'm not capable of that kind of love. But listen to the words of a fellow traveler on our planet. His name is Max . . . Christian author Max Lucado.

In his book *A Love Worth Giving,* Max writes,

> Rather than let this Scripture [on loving others] remind us of a love we cannot produce, let it remind us of a love we cannot resist—God's love. Some of you are so thirsty for this type of love. Those who should have loved you didn't. Those who could have loved you didn't. You were left at the hospital. Left at the altar. Left with an empty bed. Left with a broken heart. Left with your question "Does anybody love me?" Please listen to heaven's answer. God loves you. Personally. Powerfully. Passionately. Others have promised and have failed. But God has promised and succeeded. He loves you with an unfailing love. And his love—if you will let it— can fill you and leave you with a love worth giving.[1]

His love can free you to follow the rules. Or, rather, to follow *the* rule, that is. For there really is only one rule that rules them all . . . and that is love.

All else falls under this one command.

How can you obey the greedy demands of your English teacher and her assignments? Because to obey her is to show love. To obey her is to say, "Yes, God. I understand that maybe she's not the most lenient person with classroom assignments and due dates. And maybe diagramming sentences isn't really going to have a lot to do with me since I want to be a veterinarian someday. But, God, I'm going to trust You because You love me and You have my best interest at heart. And I trust that You are in charge of everything. You even picked this lady to be my teacher, after all. (Why, by the way, did You do that, God? Oh, sorry, never mind.) Hey, You even picked this town that I live in. You know what I need. And maybe if it's not the diagramming of prepositional phrases that I truly need from this class, maybe it's just that I need to learn how to do something that maybe I don't really want to do. Because maybe, later on, when I'm studying to be a vet, maybe I'll have to dissect an armadillo (ah! road kill!) or something; and, really, that's not all that appealing to me, especially with having to cut through the hard shell. But maybe I'll need to do it without complaining—so that I can focus and learn—because maybe that knowledge will help me when I really am a vet. It'll help me to save the life of a horse. Or a dog. Or a cat. And I'll be able to do it. And the reason why I'll be able to do it? Because I learned how to do things that I didn't want to do in my tenth grade high school English class."

It all rests under the rule of love.

Kindness does.

Obedience does.

Respect does.

All.

And this is the definition of love that He wants you to know:

Love never gives up.
Love cares more for others [even English teachers] than for self.

Love doesn't want what it doesn't have. Love doesn't strut [even in a fancy new outfit].

Doesn't have a swelled head,

Doesn't force itself on others [if Brett doesn't like you, then let him go].

Isn't always "me first,"

Doesn't fly off the handle,

Doesn't keep score of the sins of others,

Doesn't revel when others grovel,

Takes pleasure in the flowering of truth,

Puts up with anything [even little brothers],

Trusts God always,

Always looks for the best,

Never looks back,

But keeps going to the end [even until the bell actually rings].

Love never dies.

(1 Cor. 13:4–8 [with comments from the author])

You got that? If everything you do in this life is ruled by this definition of love . . . then you got it nailed, girl. You go!

And you go without fear. None. Because perfect love banishes fear (read 1 John 4:18).

Why? Because what is there to be afraid of when the strongest, smartest, bravest, most loyal One of all has your best interest in mind? Love trusts a God who is trustworthy. We trust the One who loves us. Remember the rooster? Jesus kept walking because we mean that much to Him.

> THERE IS NO ROOM IN LOVE FOR FEAR. WELL-FORMED LOVE BANISHES FEAR. SINCE FEAR IS CRIPPLING, A FEARFUL LIFE—FEAR OF DEATH, FEAR OF JUDGMENT—IS ONE NOT YET FULLY FORMED IN LOVE. (1 JOHN 4:18)

And as a result, we get to see His smile, His protection, His blessing, His favor, His joy, and His faithfulness when we trust Him.

We're going to talk more about rules and stuff as we walk through the different topics that are so important to us as teenage girls. Like clothes. And boys. And tattoos. And movies. But I'm going to warn you that you're not going to get a list of do's and don'ts from me. Nope. So if your mom bought you this book because she was hoping I was going to tell you that spaghetti-strap shirts were a definite "out," then maybe you should take it back to her and give her a hug and a sorry from me. Or, rather, why don't you finish reading it first, okay? Then take it back.

Neither am I going to tell you what shirt colors are all right and how many inches of material you need to have above your crack. Nor is it up to me to decide what base you stop at in your weekend fondling game.

It is God who decides for you with His rule of love.

Let's keep our eyes on Him rather than on the countless lists, demands, and pressures put on us by everyone else. It'll be less confusing that way.

Before we come to the end of our trail on this little chat about rules, though, I want to quickly tell you about a guy named Matt. True story. I saw it myself as it was happening on TV.

Now, Matt is a guy who has trained for years at his game. He's an athlete. He's good. He's focused. He even picked up a gold medal at the Athens Olympics just days before what I'm about to tell you.

Shooting. (Yep, it's a sport.)

Men in the shooting competition are given a target; their target sits at the end of a lane. Each competitor has his own lane. Each shot provides them with a certain number of points. Of course, as you would assume, the shooter is awarded the most number of points when he gets his shot as close to the middle of his target as possible, with the best shot being dead-on, bull's-eye, as they say.

And Matt was doing just that. He was hitting the target time after time after time.

It was the last round of shots between competitors. Matt held a comfortable lead in first place. One more decent shot from him and he'd have another gold medal placed around his neck, no matter how well his opponents performed. They wouldn't be able to catch him.

Matt loaded his gun. The room grew quiet. He lifted his gun to his shoulder. Stared at the target. Aimed. Matt's finger gently pulled the trigger. And the shot was off.

Bull's-eye.

Well, almost.

Okay, rather, on second glance . . . it wasn't a bull's-eye at all.

You see, Matt *did* hit the target. And he did place his shot in the spot that would give him enough points to win. The only problem— and it was a big problem, I might add—was that Matt had hit the wrong target. He had hit his opponent's target instead.

Big mistake for Matt.

Zero points.

Game over.

Matt left the arena, head hung low . . . in last place.

Girls, there are a lot of targets out there that you can aim for. There are a lot of things that look like the real thing, but they're not. There are a lot of people and magazines and movies telling you what a teenage girl should do, feel, say, and how much she should weigh. But they are not your targets. If you aim for them, you might hit them. You might hit straight where they want you to. But when the game is called, you will be left with nothing and everyone else will eventually walk away.

There is only one true Target. His name is Jesus Christ.

And there is only one real rule. His rule. The rule of love.

Love Him.

He loves you.

Love others.

He loves them, too.

Let every action, thought, and desire fall under this one rule of love. If you do that, I can guarantee you that you'll get the gold. And if you don't want to do that, well . . . last place is still open too.

What do you say?

Shall we go for the gold?

 GO **GIRL!**

PART 2
RAGS

CHAPTER 5

WHAT ARE YOU SAYING WITH YOUR 93 PERCENT?

He walked into the room, his identity tucked under a cap that was both beaten and bruised. His hand gripped a worn backpack hanging beside him, bumping his knee with each stride.

His jeans were torn. His face drawn taut. He made eye contact with no one.

His faded shirt appeared to have been tucked in but only part of that job still remained. He wore no belt, although it looked like he could have used one.

His shoes had been scuffed (while fleeing from the cops, perhaps? Or climbing the trash bin to rummage for food? Who knows.)

I don't think anyone had ever introduced him to a razor, either. The hair hiding his chin had most likely been cut or trimmed with scissors.

Was he hungry? Did he need food? Soap? I wanted to help him.

But he frightened me.

Granted, this was only a few months after the World Trade Center tragedy on 9/11. The post-terrorism trauma still gripped many of us in a state of suspicious fear.

He had walked into a room filled with important people. He had walked in unannounced. And, to top it off, he had gone ahead and set his backpack smack down on the floor next to the wall.

His backpack? Yes, I know.

He left it sitting there . . . alone. What was in it? Would it soon explode?

Thousands had come to this convention in Anaheim. They had gathered together for a week of media-related meetings.

This morning I sat in an area set aside for radio interviews. Waiting my turn to pop in for a hello, I grabbed a chair and passed the time impatiently thumbing through magazines and advertisements.

That is when I had seen him.

And that is when I had become afraid.

Most everyone around had taken great pains to try to look the best that they could at this event. Yet this guy looked as if he was in desperate need of a shower and a comb. Why was he there? Who had invited him? Had he come for a handout, or to blow up the Christians?

A few moments passed before I made the decision that I knew must be true.

He was a terrorist.

He had to be.

There could be no other viable explanation.

I turned to alert someone. Anyone. But who? I searched for the security guards, yet there were none to be found.

I stared at his backpack—still sitting there—looking so innocent. (They do that, you know. That's how they try to trick you . . . with the innocent-looking backpack.) But I wasn't going to be fooled. No, I would need to be the hero this time and take the backpack and toss it out the window into a fountain or a field below (were there fields in Anaheim?). Okay, maybe not. But at least I could grab it and run away from all of the other people so that no one would be harmed.

My thoughts turned to my children . . . and also to my B. While I knew that they would understand this courageous act of sacrifice I would make for thousands, I also knew that they would miss me.

And I would miss them, too.

My heart sank.

Surely there had to be another way. I considered all of my options.

Perhaps I could find someone with a cell phone and he could call the police . . . or the bomb squad. Anyone really. These things usually take time before they blast. They could tell everyone to evacuate the building before the backpack had a chance to blow. It wasn't a foolproof plan, I know, but it was worth a shot.

I stood up to try and find someone to alert, but as I did I saw the terrorist fast approaching—toward me! My heart raced like Seabiscuit at the Santa Anita.

Pounding.

Quickly.

But then I saw it. Yes—oddly enough—I saw smiles. Loads of them. And handshakes, too. One of the radio interviewers had met the man with the backpack. They were saying hello.

I slid closer, just to be there should they need anything . . . like maybe a yell for help. Anything.

But then I heard something that changed everything.

Apparently this guy wasn't a terrorist after all.

He was a singer. A musician!

In a really hip, Christian band.

Aha! I was the dunce.

It all made sense now. Now I knew why he didn't look like anyone else around. I caught on to how come he hadn't bothered to dress up for the event. He had dressed his part, the part of an artist and musician. He looked good, actually, when I saw him through those eyes. Cool jean snags.

But before I had known who he was, he had frightened me.

Why? Because his clothes and his hair and his face and his back-pack had told a story too similar to another one that could be linked to bombs and screams.

Okay, girls, I hear ya.

This walk we're taking right now is about the rags we wrap up in, not terrorism. You're probably wondering when I'm going to get to the part where I tell you how long your shorts need to be, how high your jeans need to come, and how your belly button must always, no matter what, be covered. You know that I'm going to say that, don't you? You're waiting for the hammer to fall.

Thud.

But, then again, maybe it won't.

After all, who am I to decide these things? Am I the clothing cop? Or, better yet, is there one? Where is he?

Hey, by the way, I actually like midriff shirts anyhow. I did, as a matter of fact, have an award-winning belly button in high school. Back then, though, the style was to fold down the top part of the shorts or the sweatpants when, and only when, you were in gym class or practicing dance routines after school. Come on, girls . . . you know how hot it gets when working out. And so you start to sweat. And, gee, it just really helps the ventilation to fold over the sweatpants or shorts a bit. It was purely for health reasons. You know, to air out the belly.

I liked it, though. I liked the style a lot. It was cute. It was in.

And I had the toned tummy for it. You know it.

It's just that, to be honest, I didn't quite have the heart.

But I'll explain more about that later. Right now I want to get back to the guy and the backpack—no, on second thought, let's keep him waiting a bit longer.

First, I want to tell you about the big, black breast which stared at me like the Eye of Sauron in Lord of the Rings. Yes, you read me right. No spoof. It was just one, mind you—don't get all worked up now. The other one was securely tucked away where it belonged.

I had only been in Africa for over a year so I was still pretty new about the way that things were done there. I was still pretty certain that breasts were something that needed to be . . . well, I don't know . . . covered.

But, obviously, I had a lot to learn.

She had raised her hand to ask me a question during a church talk I was giving to men and women. Her baby boy had been enjoying his drink at the start of her question but, apparently, soon got full. Or bored. Or sidetracked. Who knows. Whatever the case, his head popped off. No, not off of his body, but, rather, his head popped off of her . . . um, well . . . you know.

I wanted to interrupt her and tell her what had happened because even though *I* had noticed it, it appeared that *she* hadn't. She had just continued on with her question as if nothing had changed.

So I looked away, assuming that maybe she would catch a clue.

Nope.

Soooo . . . I thought that maybe if I drew everyone's attention to another place like with "Ah, gee, what a pretty . . . um, tree. Yeah, the tree outside the window. What a nice tree," then maybe she would take the opportunity to cover herself back up like a good girl.

Nope again.

I was getting desperate as time went on. I wanted to ask her to *please* put that thing away before someone got hurt, but as I thought about the most inoffensive way to say that, I slowly began to notice that I was the only one noticing the odd situation at all.

Then, in the midst of my strategy and planning, she stopped talking.

The room got quiet.

She had finished her question.

Uh-oh.

My turn.

Oops . . . um, what was the question again? Sorry, I had been a little distracted. But rather than having her go through the trouble of repeating it, I decided to fumble along the best I could with an answer to a question I didn't quite remember anyhow. All the while trying to direct my answer to those people in the room sitting on the other side of the big . . . well, I mean . . . of the lady.

She never did button up, actually, at least not until I was done with my answer. I think she just pretty much left it there until the kid eventually returned for dessert, I suppose.

Now, I don't know about you, but seeing a bare breast—or even two—while I'm talking about teaching children's Sunday school classes is a little unnerving. Okay, I know they're nothing new. I'm a girl myself. I've got them. I've seen them before. But, for some reason, it seems a little embarrassing, actually, to talk with someone while their . . . well, let's just say while they're not completely dressed.

But the freaky thing is—at least it was freaky to me—nobody else in the room even cared! Not even the dudes. And it was just poking out there, in midair. Full-view. I know—weird—but they didn't even bother to look. It was almost like she was nothing more to them than a bottle with arms and legs, or a leaky cup at best.

But I guess that's true.

She is.

To them.

Since then I've gotten to learn more about the culture of Kenya. And it's not that big of a deal (okay it's no big deal at all) for a girl to go topless in many parts of the country. Yep, you can walk into a village and there they all are, different shapes and sizes. And—whoa— we're talking *really* different shapes and sizes! After eight kids have nursed through those things . . . yikes!

But, oddly enough, what *would* cause an outrage in this land is if I, or any other girl, were to go out in public in shorts! And not just Charlie's Angels- or Daisy Duke-style short-shorts, either. Any shorts. Regular shorts. Gym shorts!

Yep, the knees and the thighs are the biggies here. They are the "no-no" (unlike bare breasts, of course). In fact, shorts are beyond the no-no; they're the *never*. To show them means things like prostitute, sex, erotic.

Breasts, on the other hand, mean food, entertainment for a tired toddler, and . . . well, more food!

Funny world, isn't it?

Okay, I hear you, maybe "strange" is a better word. After all, wasn't it the unveiling of Janet Jackson and her pierced . . . well, her new body jewelry at the 2004 Super Bowl halftime show, that caused such a huge outrage? Parents shrieked. Lawsuits went flying. Janet's ratings eventually suffered over all.

The scandal actually only got a small mention in the local paper in Kenya the next day. I laughed as I tried to guess how the Kenyans attempted to understand what the problem actually was. I mean, after all, breasts are viewed here with the same non-committal looks as are noses or ears or elbows or hands.

Why cover them?

Or why, if someone doesn't—as in the case of Janet—do you get so upset? I'm sure they thought, ah, those funny Americans.

The Kenyans probably never did figure out what the problem was. How could they? Because as odd as this may sound coming from a chick pulling up a chair to chat with you on things like rags and modesty (oops, I said the "m" word. Pretend you didn't hear that), the problem didn't rest entirely in what Janet did.

Nope. The boob was not the biggie.

The action, by itself, wasn't the issue. Had she done that in Zimbabwe or Timbuktu, no one would have even noticed . . . except for maybe a hungry baby nearby.

The problem, rather, came from what she meant by her infamous unveiling. Something could be read from her delayed response in covering what, to America, is normally covered. Whether you were offended or amused, her reaction spoke volumes in a language that we all understood.

Because whether you like it or not, if you live in any of the countries otherwise known as the Western world, a language has already been written about the way in which we dress.

Shirts, and how low they are, **mean something**.

Clothes, or the lack of them, **mean something**.

Rags, and how tight they are, **mean something**.

They say something loud and clear.

Not convinced? Still doubt?

Okay, pop in with me for a sec on my college communication class. What you are about to hear is bona fide true information. Documented . . . somewhere, I'm sure. Here we go. Picture this:

You are seated on the second floor of Brown Building, American College, U.S. of A. Your back hurts because the chairs in the room are left over from the Spanish Inquisition, and back then they made them straight from the bark of trees. So you're shifting from time to time, but still listening somehow. Man, you're good!

Eighteen college students sit in the room with you. You are in the third row, behind Bethany and beside Todd. Bethany and Todd are passing notes as they attempt to find out why your professor refuses to pluck his nose hairs. It's a difficult mystery to unravel, but they'll figure it out someday.

Meanwhile, you've agreed to fill them in on the day's lecture. So, you're listening. Back straight. Paying extra careful attention.

Your professor, gray beard and all, stands. He opens his mouth wide, revealing more than you had ever cared to see, and begins . . .

"Class, write this down. It will be on your quiz."

His arm slowly lifts so as to scrawl something on the whiteboard. His fingers shake ever so lightly. Then he writes, "Seven percent of all communication is done through words."

Seven percent.

Yes, you read that correctly. His hand didn't stutter.

And, no, you are not seeing a typo either in my translation of the story. The publisher did not skimp on printing and leave out a letter or two. It's not "seventy" percent. It is seven. Little ol' seven, as in the number of dwarves infatuated with Snow White. Or seven, as in the seven wonders of the world, that is before Orlando Bloom came along and made it eight.

Just seven.

That's all.

That's it.

Seven!

I know . . . you're startled. Amazed. Blown away. You begin to wonder what then makes up most of what we're saying. What do we communicate with, if it's not with our words? What counts for the 93 percent of communication that doesn't happen with our spoken vocab? And why, you ask, did you ever have to take high school English class at all if only 7 percent of communication happens with words?

It's a good question. I don't blame you for going there. But unfortunately, that's not the topic at hand. So we return, rather, to the new info, the time-bomb realization that 93 percent of who we are and what we say is not done with our words.

Nope. It's not.

Instead, your professor goes on to tell you that we talk through a form of communication called the nonverbal. Or non-gab. Or non-speak. Or non-whatever you want to call it. The distinguished man with the beard called it nonverbal, so let's leave it at that for now.

Sure, nonverbal can mean a lot of things. It's like how you tell your parents that you really don't want to go to the neighbor's house for dinner with them. But you don't say anything outright because you know they'll just disagree with you and make you go. So when it comes time to go, you're in your jammies. Your hair is a jungle. You've got your iPod blasting. And you've pasted your face with a smoothing cream.

In essence, you just said, "Mom, Dad. I love ya. But, really, can I skip out on this adult-style-dinner thing tonight? No offense, but I'd rather listen to my tunes."

It's the nonverbal.

It's how we communicate.

It's the 93 percent.

It's how you tell your best friend that you just saw Chad in the hallway and he didn't even notice you. She can see it in your eyes. She can see it in the quiver making a gentle dance on your chin.

The 93 percent.

And it's how you tell Blake, as he walks past your locker every day on his way to World History, that—yes!—you'd love to go to the pizza place with him on Friday night after the game. Even though—no—Blake doesn't quite yet remember your name.

93 percent.

No more examples. You know what that **93 percent** is about girls. You know it well.

It's called communicating without words.

We do it all of the time. Well, **93 percent** of the time.

You're a pro at doing it with your face. You pout. You smile. You give an appropriate look of hesitation . . . yeah, you know that look.

But—and it's a J-Lo sized BUT—mind you, did you ever realize how much you are actually saying with just your rags? With your choice of shirts. Colors. Jeans. Hats. Makeup. Skirts. Shoes. Socks. Sandals. Belts. Earrings. The whole bit.

They're talking.

And they're talking loudly, too.

Which brings me back, at last, to the "terrorist" and his back-pack. (I know, you thought I'd never get here. But, true to my word: I did. Phew.) The guy and the pack. His clothes said, "I don't give a tadoodle that everyone else here has conformed to an unwritten dress code of Sunday suits and polished shoes. I'm going opposite just like my music does." Well, at least that's what his clothes said to those in the room who knew him.

To me, on the other hand, they had said that he was none other than . . . yes, a terrorist. Or, okay, maybe a homeless man.

And I could have been right, you know. It wasn't such a far-fetched idea to grab. He stood out.

He said something . . . with his hair, face, and rags.

He said **something**.

But the freaky part is that depending on who was listening, he said two "somethings," really. Or even three. He said several differ-ent somethings.

Even if he didn't mean to.

Scary thought, but he's not the only one who talks like that.

We do it too.

Me.

And—yep—you! We really do.

The nine and three percent of the time.

CHAPTER 6

IT'S ALL ABOUT THE ANS

Just like the guy and the backpack, we speak a language with what we wear. We can even send out messages that we don't mean for other people to hear, yet they still hear them.

We find these outfits that really rock, trendy ensembles that are truly stylin'. We can look like the girls in the mags, have all of the right names on our tags, have all of the right rags surrounding us in a sea of style.

Our best buds love it. They hear what we're trying to say. They hear us shouting, "Look at me! I'm cool! I'm in. I'm with what's happening in this world. I'm fun to be with. Look! I'm not invisible—no way!"

They hear what we're saying and they might even agree. After all, a lot of them are trying to say the same things too. So they sympathize.

But the boys . . . the mates . . . the guys . . . the hotties. Let me tell you, gals, they're hearing something a lot different than that. Just like I misread Mr. Terrorist Musician, a lot of these guys are misreading you.

They see you in your tank. They see you in your shorts. They see you in your full-length body glove. Now—catch it—they're not thinking, "Oh, Stacy looks so cute today! How sweet!"

Nope. (Although you do look cool, Stacy, but that's not my point.)

Rather the guys are thinking, "Whoa! Stace-babe . . . Stace! Staaacyyyy. You got some over the summer. How about coming over here, Stace. I accidentally dropped my pencil. Oops. Man, I'm a klutz. Do you think you could bend over and pick it up for me? Slowly?"

Yes, that's the guy's take on your total tank.

But my outfit is cute, you shout back. And cleavage happens to be in right now. It's fashion. Who ever said it was against the law to dress in style? It's not my fault that guys' brains are swimming where they shouldn't. Maybe they just need to grow up. Do I have to dress like Mary Poppins just because some guys have a gutter for a mind? Anyhow, I don't believe it. The guys who think that way are scum. The guys I know would never think those thoughts. They're Christian guys. They're cool. They like my outfits.

Yes, I answer back.

They do. They like what you are wearing. Or, at least, a part of them does. But I'm sorry to be the one to burst your Pollyanna bubble—really, I am—it's just that it's not the part of them that you want. It's not the part of them that will remember the real you past tomorrow.

Yes, your outfit might be cute. I agree with you on that. But guys are coming from a different planet than "cute." They might speak our language, sure, and even say, "Hey, cuuuuttte outfit." But they're not thinking "cute," nor are they thinking anymore about you, at least not about the *you* that really matters.

And what's worse, it's not just the guys whose attention you want who are looking at you now. It's that gutter-scum, too. Why, these perverts might even include grandpa's fishing buddies. Or the bus driver. Or the boys at school who blow their noses on porno mags. How about the deacon at church who sings in the choir and gives you a smile when no one else is looking? Even your math teacher is a candidate . . . and who knows who else!

Gross, you say?

Tell me about it!

But the list continues. Dare I go on? Okay, okay. You get the pic.

So what do we do? Line up all of the guys in the world and shoot them? At least that way we can wear whatever we want without having to worry about being eaten up for dinner by some crude guy in his mind.

So it's settled. **We shoot them.**

Okay, let's not. Bad idea. The lads have their problems for sure, but overall they're kind of nice to have around. I know I can't stand it a day without B. He's my best friend.

But what do we do?

Just steer clear of gutter-scum?

Not as easy as it sounds. They often come disguised, you know.

Perhaps, then, we really do need to examine this rag deal a bit more.

[HENRY TALKS]

Hey girls. I got a little nervous when Heather started talking about lining up all of the guys in the world and shooting them. So I was thinking that it might be a good time for me to explain my breed. Fine by you? Hope so, because here goes!

Agreed upon point: each individual communicates nonstop every day without ever opening our mouths. And clothes are one of the ways we chit-chat. The problem is that guys don't always hear the same thing that you are saying.

Guys and girls are different. We don't look alike. We don't eat alike. We don't think alike. And we don't do things alike. Take going to the restroom, for example. We have no problem going by ourselves. You, on the other hand, think it's a team sport!

But guys and girls think differently about more things than just day outings to the restroom. We think differently about life—what we see, what we hear. We interpret things differently. We just do.

Let's say you don a tight outfit thinking it's just an all-the-way sweet look. Well, to a guy who is looking at you, it may **be** all-the-way sweet, but not for the right reasons. And, trust me, you don't want a guy to think **that** about you. You want him to be about you for the right reasons. So what's a girl to do?

My advice: leave some mystery in the air. Don't dress the tease.

Guys dig mystery. We love the chase. Just check out all of the conquests in history. It's guys going out to explore. We see something, and we explore it.

Which brings me to my next point. Guys are different from girls in that we are also very visually stimulated. Now, keep in mind that the exploring aspect is still there. When a guy sees a slit of underwear or a bra strap sticking out, or a tattoo on the lower back peeking out above the jeans, his mind doesn't stop there. That tidbit only gets him thinking about what else is there. He wants to explore. So he connects the dots and fills in the blanks—all by his little ol' self—in his mind.

Guys are entirely visual! In Genesis 29, when Jacob sees Rachel for the first time, he weeps. Why? The answer is in verse 17: "Rachel was beautiful of form and face" (NASB).

Now *form* is just a nice word for . . . well, you can figure that out!

Jacob was visual.

Rachel was beautiful.

Jacob wept.

On January 22, 2005, Donald Trump, the billionaire tycoon and *Apprentice* star with the tidal wave hairdo, married Melania, a lady whom many people consider "beautiful of form and face." Trump knows men. He knows what they're thinking when they see her. He once said about her, "When we walk into a restaurant, I watch grown men weep."[1]

We're visual.

It's the way we're made.

Sure guys are visual, Uncle H. I hear you on that. I've seen it already!

I was at a rock concert once way back in my day (the singer's probably a grandpa now), and this girl decided to get on the stage and dance with the star while he sang.

Pretty soon her shirt came off. (Gee, how did that happen? Must have gotten snagged on the microphone stand, I guess. Poor thing.) Anyhow, she somehow managed to keep dancing. What a true fan!

And I can tell you that when she did, the stadium full of screaming onlookers (at least the guy portion of them) didn't really care so much anymore about the singer they had paid through the nose to come and see.

All eyes were now on the girl.

Let me help explain this phenomenon with a bit of biology. Yes, I know . . . eewww, yuck. I'm not a big biology fan either, but there's some biology stuff that pertains to us, and sometimes it helps us to know it. You see our bodies are made with different systems: breathing, digestion. . . . You get the point.

One of these systems was given to us as an alert system. It functions as an internal alarm to alert us when there is danger, pain, or arousal, among other things. It's called the "autonomic nervous system," the ANS.

It's kind of like when you are in the car and another car is suddenly coming straight at you (or you are heading for a concrete wall), and you think for a split second, "Huh, I won't have to turn in my math assignment tomorrow because the end of all things has finally come." The hair on the back of your neck stands up and sings Dixie. Your heart beats so fast that you shut your mouth so it can't jump out. Droplets of sweat dash across your forehead.

That's the proud work of the ANS doing its job.

The brain is actually sending small but mighty messengers throughout your body.

Now, we all have the ANS, sure. It's just that the guys' ANS also includes a part that is prompted by the visual . . . like with the topless girl dancing at the concert.

ANS!

So, yes, a topless chick can activate the ANS. True. But to be honest, gals, it doesn't take all that much to do so. If a dude sees you walking by having trouble breathing because your shirt is two sizes too small . . . righto. ANS! And yes, this is true even if he's a Christian. Last I checked, Christian dudes still have a central nervous system.

It's hard for us to understand this since we're not so visually aroused. But for a guy, that ANS is screeching loud and clear, pretty much most of the time. And we need to be aware of it, for our sake as well as for the guys. Why? Because even on their best days, guys are guys, and they were created to be visual beings. And it would be good if we could try to remember that. And approach them that way, especially if you want to have a relationship one day with a guy that actually means something.

We can't always put everything off on them. Sure, they have their side of the deal, but we have to be real about ours as well.

And one way we can be real is in what rags we grab. What do you say with what you're wearing? Do you copy the style of scanty and say, "Use me. I'm not worth much; there is nothing else here for you to discover." Or do we go for another style that says, "There's someone standing in front of you who is the total package. Whole. Here. And a lot more than you could ever find out. Just try."

Guys may have scanty for a small snack, but they take the mystery for the long run. They dig the discovery. They may salivate over skin, but last I checked, a guy's heart isn't in his tongue.

Don't sell yourself short. Once you do, remember that for the guy the game's over. He sits up, burps, and moves on.

[BRIAN TALKS]

You know, ladies. It's hard to re-create the mystery once you've lost it. Once you've unveiled the package, you can't wrap it back up again.

Guys—the good ones—really dig a girl with dignity, someone who knows they are worth something and they dress like it. How can that be, you ask, especially when all the girls who get the most attention are the ones who forget to wear a bra that day?

Well sure, they do get the looks, but when everything has been displayed there is nothing left for the guy to pursue. So he just moves on. This may sound strange, but anything that comes quick and easy is just not worth having. Sure, the short-term looks are hard to pass up, but, girls, you want what is real and what will last.

The truth is, we think we can tell the depth of your character by the way you dress. Maybe we're wrong. But we think it nonetheless. Maybe this will make sense: your rags tell guys how close you are to going further with them. Yikes! That is really brash sounding, but in a way it is true. Whatever you expose with what you wear takes a guy's mind one step closer to how he pictures you naked. The more you show, the less he has to imagine.

Of course, not all guys let their minds have full reign like this. But I can assure you of this, the ones who are attracted to girls who dress with dignity are the ones who will really take care of you. They are real men with real hearts! And you are worth having that type of guy, and that kind of relationship won't leave you heartbroken and crying.

Get a load of this one reporter's take on Britney Spears, child star turned pop diva, for example. It totally reaffirms exactly what we've been talking about—straight from the mouth of a dude.

MSNBC contributor Michael Ventre said,

It seems Britney Spears is set to appear in the September [2005] issue of British *Elle* wearing little beyond a belly button bauble and a swatch of denim. . . . Ordinarily, I wouldn't bat an eye when a pop star of Britney's stature decides that a career jolt is needed and the best way to achieve that is a foray into soft porn. . . . But this is the real crossroads for Britney. By baring all, she is serving notice that she has nothing left.[2]

Nothing.

Nothing left.

No mystery.

None at all.

Her notice that she has nothing left has a two-fold message: one, that she doesn't think her voice, dance, or charisma is enough to carry her so she's turning to what will, at least for the moment, draw drools; two, she has nothing left to unveil. A year or two, or even three, of guys chewing her as cud, and then they'll be full. She'll either have to reinvent herself in a pure, mystical sort of way—kind of what Madonna tried to do when she transformed herself from the "boy-toy" persona into the "material girl" over a decade ago—or Britney will be done.

She'll have to re-create the mystery. Or call it quits.

But, you know what? It can be done.

You can do it!

You can start again.

You can start now.

No accusations here, but check it: let's just say that perhaps from time to time you've been dressing the ho—er . . . the in style, I mean. Maybe you don't realize it, but maybe you make for good locker room laughs. Or it could be that your choir teacher gives you extra attention and always calls on you when you raise your hand, and he especially holds tight those frontal hugs . . . and for a long time.

Don't buy into this momentary interest.

You are worth so much more than a moment. Make people remember you for who you are, your essence, your wit, your worth, your sparkle.

Re-create the mystery.

You can.

Please, try.

Not just for yourself.

But, hey, why not also think of the guys?

[HENRY TALKS]

You know what, ladies? I would be so grateful if you thought of us. Because here's the truth, my young friends: Christian guys do want to walk in obedience to Christ. Yet, sadly, one of the areas where too many guys fall is in the area of lust. We get the temptations in a lot of places: billboards, newspaper inserts, the Internet . . .

And with the way a girl dresses.

I'm not trying to lay down a law on what is too short or too low or too tight by jumping into the equation here. I am, however, hoping that you will remember the one rule that rules them all. Remember what Heather talked about earlier?

Love.

She told you what love actually is, straight from the Bible in 1 Corinthians 13. Remember how the passage said we could live and show love?

"Love cares more for others than for self."

And one way of putting it is . . .

Kindness is looking out for someone else's needs ahead of yours, like not being mean, or a tease, or a temptation.

Please, I beg you, be kind.

I believe that being kind in how you dress *is* love.

I also believe that most of you honestly don't realize the struggle you place before guys with some of your choices of style. But that struggle is there, regardless. I frequently give talks to teen boys and men about porn and lust and other guy issues. Do you realize what they tell me is most often the battle for them? It's not the movies. It's not the magazines.

It is the way that girls dress.

Their rags at school, at work, even at church.

You know, it happened to me. I remember sitting behind a girl at church who was probably around seventeen. Before the service started, she leaned forward to talk to the person in front of her and I got caught off guard. In plain sight was two inches of her underwear. Remember the ANS? Well, I don't really remember the sermon from that day, but I still remember what I saw.

You see, guys are visual—we just are. Especially when the ANS has been alerted. You say, hey, what's the big deal? It's just two inches of underwear. She's still covered. But for us it's about what the underwear means. Things don't stop there. There is a natural reaction in guys to want to explore the rest. A bra strap showing leads to where the rest of that bra strap might go. Two inches of underwear does the same thing. It's not nearly as innocent as what you might think.

So on behalf of Christian chums worldwide, I ask you—no, I beg you—be kind.

Love.

For some reason, I've got this feeling that you're still squirming a bit. Maybe I've got that feeling because I know that to talk about style pushes a button. Because it could just be that you like the looks too much. Maybe you like the momentary glances, the extra attention, the power . . . and the control.

Will you get attention if you dress the rage? Yes. But to be honest, it's not the kind of attention that will benefit you overall. Nor will it benefit the guy who is giving it. Rather, the real you will soon be lost in lust, chewed up, digested, and then forgotten. You will be remembered only as a taste. A morsel stuck between his teeth somehow. He'll pick you out with a toothpick and then spit.

You are more than a morsel, girl! Don't settle for morsel! No way! Don't do it!

Mystery makes guys remember you for the right reasons. And it makes them remember *all* of you.

Go with it.

Don't give in like so many girls have. Don't throw yourself away for the quick nod and the wave. Make them want to get to know you longer than the commercial . . . the real you . . . not another bimbo.

Gnaw a moment on these words from former Mickey Mouse Club singer turned sex icon, Christina Aguilera. She said this in 1999, before she took her slide into skimpy:

> It's important to me to be a positive role model. Parading around in my bra and a pair of hot pants will not inspire confidence in other girls. That would just make me one more person pushing them to feel like they have to be something they're not. I'm not just another bimbo. I've got a brain and a heart. And I'm not gonna let my body distract people from that fact.[3]

Well . . . um, Christina, the world stands distracted.

And, unfortunately, not just by her anymore, but by girls at school, at work, on the street. And even at church and in youth groups.

But do you know what the shame of it all really is? Do you know where my gripe really comes from? It's that Christina's not truly a bimbo. She's not. Even if the world has forgotten that.

And, what's more, neither are you.

So why dress like one?

Come on—don't we have it hard enough as it is to be taken seriously on this planet? Do we really need to encourage the stereotypes and assumptions? We have a brain. And we have a heart . . . heart enough to know what real love is. Heart enough to know how to show it.

Heart enough to know that it isn't love to flaunt something in front of a guy that he can't enjoy without sinning. If you want to dress that way with your life-long mate, your hubby, your catch one day, I say, go for it, girl! Go get him! Go on!

But to dress the tease because you dig the attention . . . well, to be honest, that's mean.

Not loving.

Not kind.

Not trusting God enough to follow His one, solitary call: ***love***.

What say you, then?

Do we take it up a notch and choose our rags with both worth and kindness in mind? Or do we remain content to continue the cycle of temptation and tease, encouraging our brothers to stumble while cheapening our own self-esteem.

Go higher than that, girlfriend.

Jump.

Take the leap.

You really can soar if you try.

Go on.

Give it a go.

Why not try *love* on for size?

CHAPTER 7

LOOKING FOR SOMETHING

Tripping in my twenties, I hadn't yet grasped the truths so many younger Christians seem to know. I was married and had two tikes already. Yes, two. The bellybutton had gone there and back again twice. But I was still searching. Still looking.

I had signed up to tryout for my city's professional football team's cheerleading squad. Six hundred other hopeful girls had signed up with me. We had all met together in the football team's practice gymnasium. We learned the steps. We made the moves. We tried to charm the judges with our smiles.

Every few hours some of us would be asked to leave. Names were called. Dreams were dashed. And the number dwindled down.

500. 400. 300. 200. And so on.

The next day came.

There were only ninety of us left by then. We were tired but somehow managed to push on with the help of adrenaline (this was before Red Bulls!). We danced. They judged. Only thirty-three would eventually be chosen.

While I remember a lot of things from that time, like the dance coach, the music, the other girls, the heartbreak in hearing that they were now tossing ballet-like leaps and stuff (oh thrill!) into the final routine—so as to separate those who really did have dance training from the ones, like me, who were faking it—I also remember the crushing disappointment of not hearing my name in the final thirty-three—*ouch*. But there is something else that I remember even stronger.

Funny enough, but true, it was a guy. My boss, actually. I had been working under him at the time doing speaking in local schools and stuff. I sat in his office about a week before tryouts and told him about my grand idea. I remember thinking how happy he must be for me and how cool he would think it would be to have a professional cheerleader working under him, should I make it.

But what I remember more, actually, is how wrong I had been about that.

Because he didn't like my idea at all.

Instead, he just got kind of quiet at first. And then he asked me why I felt like I needed to do it. Didn't I have enough to do already? He couldn't seem to understand why I didn't value who I was that I felt like I had to dance half-naked in front of 60,000 football fans to feel complete.

"You don't have to do this, Heather," he said, his eyes outlined in a sympathy I had never yet seen. "You don't have to do this. You know that, don't you?"

Sorry to say, but I didn't know that.

I wish that I had.

I really do.

But I didn't.

Not then.

What is it within us that longs for attention? Why do we feel that we don't matter unless we belong? Why must we continually thumb through our closets looking for just the right outfit that will draw the attention. The looks. The acceptance. Why is it so hard to believe that we're enough as we are, to realize that a soul and a spirit and a sparkle mean so much more than an illusion of status and style.

You know, we don't just dress for the guys, do we, gals? We do it for each other, too. We long for that security which comes from attention. We long to be better than the next person. We thrive on competition. We want to show Ashley that we know where and how to shop. We want Beth to know that we have the eye to pick out the best top. We want the girls to notice and somehow believe that because we dress really cool, we must *be* cool.

We live for the compliments. We live for the looks.

We hide insecurities. We cover up holes. We wrap ourselves in an image, disguising our faults. And, don't get me wrong, I'm not bashing looking your best. I think you should. I think I should. We are a reflection of God's love, and we are His creation. We need to accept that and show that to others and be glad in it ourselves, have fun with it, even.

But a lot of the styles today—and also in my day, sure—have asked us to compromise who we really are. They ask us to hop up on the stage and let every Tom, Dick, and Jeremy enjoy his eye-fill.

So we reason it away. We justify things in our minds. I know I did. A lot. We tell ourselves that we're just dressing like this because it's really cute, when, truth out, it's hot. But we ignore that. We stick with cute. And it's good to look cute. Who wants to blend into the wall? It's not such a bad thing to stand out. Anyhow, we say, God just looks at the heart. He doesn't really care what I'm wearing as long as I'm not trying to be a bad person or a ho.

And you're right. The Bible tells us clearly that "man looks at the outside but God sees the heart."

But, in fact, that *is* our problem.

That's it.

God sees our hearts.

There is more to a person's heart than just her intentions, you know? There's more than just, "I don't want someone to lust over me or be jealous and feel intimidated by me, but I'm going to wear this outfit anyhow and they should know that if they do feel that way, it's their own fault. Not mine."

God sees more than that.

Deep in our hearts are also our motivations. Our desires. Our dreams.

When we use something God has given us—example being our bodies or looks—to draw attention to ourselves above others, not to mention above God, our hearts are being selfish. Our motivation is definitely not to honor God or to stroll with Him like He asks.

Rather, it's to get attention. Or control. Recognition.

Some of us try to do this by talking louder than everyone else. Others do it with a really wild laugh. Some of us try to do it by cutting ourselves or pretending that we're hurt or sick. Some through starving. Lying. It doesn't matter what we use to try and do it—God sees our hearts.

He sees past our clothes, our cuts, and the absence of food on our plates, and He sees the same heart. A heart that is anemic in faith, a heart that refuses to trust God with her relationships, her purpose, her value, and her life.

It all boils down to whether or not we're going to trust Him and whether or not we're going to let Him take His proper place on our center stage. It matters whether or not we're going to believe Him enough that we would risk losing what we think we want in order to receive what He has, to receive what comes when we let go of our own approach and rest, instead, in His plans for us. In His mandate of love. Because another part of loving is something called being humble. And no, I'm not talking about a pig named Wilbur and his spider friend Charlotte.

I'm talking humble.

H—U—M—B—L—E.

New word here.

Humble means accepting who God made us to be and not trying to promote ourselves as something better than what we are, not trying to dress the part of the Hollywood actress or pop-star. You know, truth be said, they're dressing a part, too. They're just playing a role. Because after the lights turn off and the camera shuts down, they're only humans with faults, fears, and failures, who also just so happen to pee, vomit, and bleed . . . like me and you.

Dressing with humility means letting go of the need to impress, letting go of the need to have the smallest jean size. Or the largest breasts. Or the most guys' heads turning in the hall when you walk with your friends. It's allowing someone else to shine, without being jealous. It's allowing other people to talk, without interrupting.

It's a big role. I know. I'm not asking you to do anything that I haven't asked myself as well. It's hard. I mean, how do we know that God's plan is going to be enough, anyhow? How do we know, if we don't try to dress for ourselves, that we'll even have friends at all? How do we know that we can trust Him?

How do we know that He even cares?

Do you remember when I told you earlier that I had the toned tummy for the fold-over sweats but that I didn't have the heart for it? This is what I meant: I didn't have a heart that would trust God above herself. A heart willing to take second seat so that Someone else can be first. Rather, I opted for the momentary attention, the longer and lingering conversations, making the other gals who didn't have such toned tummies jealous. I liked the illusion of control that came with all of that.

But God saw my heart.

He saw that I needed many lessons yet in learning how to trust Him, and crimminy-picket, lessons hurt! He saw that I was holding on to my own will because I thought it was the only thing that could get me where I wanted to go.

Sure, I wasn't trying to entice a guy or sell myself as a hussy on the streets of a big city. But He still saw a heart that was pretty ugly, crawling with doubt. Untrusting of Him. Aloof.

To dress "cute" yet still covered in a way that isn't going to draw looks or drools means you really have to let go and trust that God loves you and that He will provide the kind of attention, affirmation, and acknowledgment that you need as a girl.

That can be scary. And it feels risky, too . . . kind of like jumping off that platform above the river Nile. What if it doesn't work? What if I fall headfirst into the hippos and the crocodiles? How do I know that I can trust Him? Especially when I don't always see girls suffering by getting attention in the wrong way. Especially when I can't see their hearts and the empty tears inside. I can only see the smiles. And the makeup under which they try to hide.

Stepping out in faith, like stepping off the platform, means trusting God for something by doing what He says even, or especially, when you don't see how it is possible that it will work out in the end.

I hate this more than you do.

I must be the biggest bum when it comes to the faith thing. (Yeah, I know, so why am *I* writing this book to you? Don't know. Ask the publisher! They asked me to!) I mean, for me, I'm like, okay, God, show me *first* how You're going to do this or that or the other. And then I'll follow You.

Show me first.

Show me how that if I do the right thing—like drop this dude who has acted like a pretty decent friend for a long time but recently started eating me with his eyes and then asked me to do something I shouldn't—You'll fill the gap that he leaves behind. Last I checked, there wasn't a row of dudes lining up to apply for the role to be my pal. Come on, God.

Show me that if I let go of ambition and pride and dress in a manner that reflects contentment and worth and kindness, that there'll even be anyone who wants to talk to me at all. They won't. I'm only good for being used. I've learned that over time.

Or, at least, I've learned to believe the lie.

Many of us do.

We believe the lie.

Do you?

Lies are easy to believe. Unfortunately.

CHAPTER 8

TRADING THEM IN

Morgan is five. She loves to dress up and pretend that she is a princess. She loves jewelry, too, especially this one necklace that she got out of a bin at a pizza and game place when she was three. She's taken it with her everywhere. It's either in her little princess bag or around her neck. She loves it.

Now, Morgan doesn't yet realize that her necklace is actually just made up of plastic and string. She hasn't yet discovered that with one strong yank from her little brother the whole thing would break. She doesn't understand how the clasp, when she wears it, actually turns her neck green.

Morgan loves her necklace, because that's all Morgan has ever seen.

One day, Morgan's daddy came home from a trip that his business sent him on to New York City. Over the years, he had witnessed her attachment to her dime-store jewelry. On this trip, he decided to get Morgan the real thing so that when the day finally came that she grew up, she would still have the treasure of her dreams. It wouldn't have faded. It wouldn't have broken.

Because it was real.

Morgan's dad hailed the cab and took off in it for Tiffany and Co. He paid the cash. And bought Morgan a necklace fit for a queen.

It's just that Morgan's daddy needed her to give him her plastic necklace first. He didn't want her to confuse them. He wanted her to eventually forget the cheap one and replace it with the new one that would last.

"Give me your necklace, Morgan," Daddy said as he held out the gift, all tied up in a box with a red ribbon. "I have something for you. Something good. A gift for a princess. A gift for forever. And for always, too."

"No, Daddy," Morgan cried. "I want my necklace. I won't give it to you. I don't want your box with wrapping and ribbons. Keep it. I've got what I want. That's all that I need."

"Give me your necklace, Morgan," Daddy said again, tears filling his eyes. He understood his girl's attachment. He understood that she was afraid to give up what she knew for that which she didn't. But he wanted her to trust him. He wanted her to see that she could. So he waited. He waited for her to give him her necklace first.

"No, Daddy," Morgan said, gripping her plastic jewels even tighter. "You can't have them. I want them. They're mine. Please go. And take your box with you."

Morgan's daddy left her room that night a sad man. Morgan never did exchange her Mardi Gras imitation for the shimmering gift. He couldn't force her to do so, not if he wanted her to learn the most important thing, which is to decide on her own.

A few months went by and Morgan picked up her fake necklace to wear it. The string that held the beads together had weakened over use and time. It snapped as she fastened it around her neck, the small pieces falling and rolling away.

Morgan quickly ran to her daddy, sobbing. He held her and wiped her tears as they came. Eventually, she opened her small hand revealing the few pieces of her necklace that she had managed to find.

Her daddy took them, gently, and put them in his pocket. Setting her down for a moment, he went to the shelf. Pulling off a small box, he then returned and placed it in her hand, still wrapped and tied with a red ribbon.

Morgan's dad was glad that she had finally asked him for it, but he was sad for the pain and loss that she had to feel first in order to do so. He wished, instead, that she had simply trusted him and traded with him, on the night of his offer, her plastic impression for his genuine gem.

But that takes faith. Doesn't it?

That, by definition, is what faith is. Faith is to believe in something that you cannot see. The Bible tells us that God is pleased by our faith. He is touched when we have faith. Abraham and others were made righteous even by their faith, not because they saw how it would all work out good in the end, but because they believed God was true, truthful, and good. They believed Him, in spite of how things looked, and so they followed.

I can't give you an answer that you can see to the questions that plague both you and me. I can only say that I've tried myself, and I don't work. I've tried the world, and it doesn't work either. I've tried reason, and it falls short, with an added sting. I've even tried good intentions, and they somehow fail too.

But when I've tried God, He has never left me lacking any good thing.

It takes faith. From inside. In the heart.

Because God doesn't buy it when we just do the actions to test Him and then accuse Him of not being there for us.

No, that won't work.

It's only when we commit our hearts to trusting Him—and truly obey His way, come what may—that He will lift us up to where we can soar.

He's asking us to exchange the magazine's lie of what a girl should dress like, for His truth. He's asking us to trade an image for something that will last. Will you give Him a go? A *real* go, that is?

You want to know something? There's someone else who is willing to trade with you as well. He wants your heart and a say-so on your clothes. And he will tell you the things that you want to hear in order to get it. Because he's a liar. And a thief. And a snake. And if you go with him, he'll also give you an exchange.

Your life. Your hope. Your sparkle. Your shine.

For shame.

Because after the so-called friends have gone home and the rags you used to catch them lie tossed and used in the basket, stained, only the memories of what was traded remain.

You gave yourself.

In return, you got shame.

Shame is kind of like embarrassment. It's how you feel after you've hurt someone you care about. It's how you feel after you've given yourself to someone who didn't really care about you. We all have it. We can push it aside, sure. But it's still there.

The telling words of Britney Spears, after a photo shoot where she wasn't exactly what most would call a mystery (seeing as she was naked from the waist down), can sadly bring it all to light:

> I did feel kind of weird after those photos. I was in a moment. I had, like, eight Red Bulls and said, "OK, let's do it." I learned my lesson and you won't see me like that for a while. . . . It is really revealing and I wouldn't want my kid, at 21, to be dressing like that.[1]

Sure, Red Bulls or whatever can get us through a moment. But when the Bull bows out, we realize what we've done. And deep down, we all know when we've been used. We all know when we preferred the words, the attention, the looks, the snap of the shutter, and the lies about ourselves . . . and so we traded something—our dignity, our respect, our skin—for shame.

We've been used.

We didn't care if 60,000 people in the stands were going to see us dancing around only a wee-bit covered. We didn't care if half of them might have us for lunch later in the shower and get off on what they saw. We wanted to belong.

To what?

Anything that would have us.

Because we refused to trust the One to whom we already did belong.

So we offered ourselves cheaply.

Only to discover that when sixty minutes and four quarters had ended, guess what?

Game's done.

Stuff the outfit and the smile in the locker.

Go home.

The 93 percent had said, "Use me. I'm not worth much anyhow."

Oh, but if you're thinking that right now, then I really beg to differ. I do.

Because you are worth so much more.

Did you hear me? I said, you truly *are!*

I wish I could stand atop the tallest tower on the most mammoth of mountains and shout with the lungs of a lion, *you are worth so much more!*

But I can't, sorry. I'm a bit lung-deficient and have low blood pressure that could cause me to pass out in high altitudes . . . not a pretty sight.

Anyhow, I don't need to, because Someone else already did.

There is Someone who already climbed the mountain, all of the steps of the hill called the Skull. There is Someone else who already roared so loudly that He actually tore a temple curtain in two. There is Someone else who already proved that you are worth it and, because of that, has nothing but the very best of intentions and plans for you.

You can trust Him.

You can believe Him.

He proved it already. On the cross.

He will catch you if you trust Him. He will exchange what you give Him for what you truly want. A real love. A lasting acceptance. Security. And, what's more, shame won't be part of the deal.

The thing is, when the Israelite people were told to make sacrifices to God in the Old Testament times, they were told to slaughter lambs and goats and bring different offerings. Once a year, on the Day of Atonement for sin, the priest had to do something extra special. He had to pick a goat—a pure and perfect one—and he had to put his hands on it. With his hands on the goat, the priest then symbolically transferred the shame of the people to it. The goat was then later sent out, outside of the city walls, abandoned and left to wander, starve, and die a slow and painful death. Alone.

The purpose of this particular scapegoat was to take away the shame that the people felt.

God remembered that goat, and our shame, you know, when it came time for the ultimate. When it came time for the Christ.

You see, Jesus died on a cross, sure. But did you ever realize that His slow and painful death occurred outside the city walls? Abandoned by God and man? Just like the goat led out to die for the shame of the people, Jesus not only shed His blood for us but He hung there, alone, for our shame.

He hung there naked . . . so that we wouldn't have to.

He uncovered Himself to tell us that we are worth covering up. You are worth it.

You really are.

Bask in the attention of the One who says so. Seek the affection of those He has for you. You are worth the genuine interest, love, and friendship that develops in the context of trust between people who want to be with you for who you are . . . not for what you will supply their eyes for a moment.

Believe it.

Own it.

Wear it, a badge of beauty on a body of grace.

Go on, girls. Grasp it.

Grasp the truth of your rightful place, a girl clothed in mystery, adorned with her worth from above.

PART 3

RELATIONSHIPS

CHAPTER 9

DESPERATE

Girlfriends.

Pals.

ALLIES.

Cliques.

Divas.

Snobs.

`Mean girls.`

Sum it up? We've got them all, don't we? We've got the whole kit-and-caboodle. We've got our girls who we hang with every day, the ones we plan our futures with, including our trek through Europe that we'll take together one day. We go shopping with these girls, watch movies, and never so much as hint at a catfight.

Then there are the others, the mean girls. These are the girls we know must be packing fangs underneath their Hollywood grins. They are cats, clawers, climbers. They're users. Snitches.

Welcome to Planet World, because we're all here.

Like Bilbo Baggins of *Lord of the Rings* says, "It's a dangerous business going out your front door. . . ."

'Cause you never know what you're going to run into. You never know who you're going to end up sitting next to in art class. You never know who your mama's going to invite over for you to chill with because she's become good friends with her mama. You never know who else is going to make the soccer team. Or the drill team. Or the cooking team . . . if there is one. But you get my point.

Life is an open game. Everyone gets a turn to play. And play together.

The challenge comes in learning how to do it. And how to do it well.

Oh, I hear you, there are some of you reading this who think that maybe it's a lost cause. You want to toss in the towel, grab a flight to Alaska someday and surround yourself with polar bears and huskies. You've had it with getting burned, forgotten, talked about, let down, or used.

But it won't work.

Sorry.

Once school is over (and yes, contrary to what you might believe right now, it will someday be over) you will work. You will be around the people you work with. Or you will get married. Go to church. You will buy groceries or fast food. Rent movies. Whatever.

You will be with people.

You will *relate* to them.

Aha! You will have relate-tionships.

And, what's more, you will need them.

Here's the deal: God made us in His own image.

Yep. You know that. We're told that. He made us in His own style, with His own way of looking at things.

He made us for relationships.

Why?

Because God craves relationships.

He craves them so much that He dug the first one out of the dirt of the ground, and that would be Adam. If God didn't want relationships, He would have settled for his cool troupe of angels surrounding Him with songs of "Holy, holy, holy."

But He didn't.

He wanted more.

So . . . voilà . . . He made us!

Maybe He made us because He wanted to be able to see someone smile at Him who didn't really have to. Or maybe because He wanted to see someone trust Him who had another option from which to choose. Maybe He wanted to tell us some of His fanciful or freaky stories, and He wanted us to tell Him our stories, too—while we lived them (that's what we call "prayer").

God made us.

He didn't have to.

But He did.

And, what's more, He made us knowing full well that there was going to be a pretty steep price tag on the label. Yet, He still made us. And then He paid it—cha-ching.

Because relationships really do matter.

God wants them. And, last I checked, if you're human, and got the DNA to prove it, the belly button, and the unique little thumbprint, you were made in the image of God.

Thus, a therefore: You need relationships, too.

You crave them. We all do. Friendships. Camaraderie. Someone to encourage and guide us. Someone to just pass time with. Someone to make us laugh. Or someone to tell us that our naturally curly hair looks great, even though "straight" has been in forever.

We need each other. We really do, even if we try to convince ourselves otherwise.

Which, admit it, we sometimes try.

Hey. Ever heard of the boxer Muhammad Ali? If you've never seen him, I'm sure you've heard about him. At the very least, you know Will Smith, and Will played Ali in a movie in 2001.

Well, back in his day, Ali was it. He was on top. He was tight. He was sweet.

And he knew it.

Like most boxers, Ali had nicknames to go with his game. Some called him the King. Others called him . . . shhh, quiet on the set, eh-hem . . . Superman.

One day—true tale—Ali was on a plane. The stewardess came over to him and reminded him that he needed to buckle up since they were about to land.

Ali replied with a smug grin, "Superman doesn't need a seatbelt."

The stewardess, gearing up for her own quick jab, leaned over and replied, "I said buckle up. Because Superman doesn't need a plane to fly."

Rather than accept the reality of who he truly was, Ali believed a lie. Sure, he could pack a punch or two, but he wasn't any Superman.

And, sorry to say, neither are you.

Nor am I.

We can't go it alone. We were made for relationships. We need friends. Real ones. Not just posters on our walls. Or pictures to trade. Yearbooks to sign. Or a youth group to meet with for an hour each Wednesday.

We need friends.

Real ones.

A buddy.

A pal.

A best friend forever.

We need girls we can go-to and go-through anything with. The Bible tells us that three strands of a chord are not easily broken. This being so, the strands of true friendship make us stronger, snappier, and smarter in a world full of zips and bumbles.

So how do we go about this whole girlfriend thing then? Do we just hold open-auditions and anyone who applies gets chosen?

Hmmmm . . . maybe not.

See, I had to do that once.

Not fun. In fact, it was more than not fun. It was a nightmare.

Let me tell you about it.

In college, I was casting an original play that I would be direct-ing. I had handpicked a great script, so I was really psyched about the whole thing. The rift came in that one of the parts was written for a younger-looking high school girl. So I came up with the idea of narrowing the casting of that character to a real high-school student, not just someone who could gear-down in age.

It's just that while my idea was pretty grand, my advertising lurked more around lousy. I think I sent a solitary memo off to one high school drama coach in the entire city. Talk about non-overkill. So guess what? Yep! My open auditions for high school students drew a sum total of . . . um, one!

One. That's it.

And I asked her, **"Can you read?"**

"Yes."

"Can you talk?"

"Yes."

"Can you breathe?"

"Yes."

"Okay. I pick you!"

Thankfully for me and for the rest of the crew, she was good and the play ended up performing to decent reviews. But it could have bombed. It could have been that the only gal to show up didn't know the first thing about acting or the stage. Even still, I would have had to cast her. If she had arrived, and she was able to walk, talk, and smile, she'd be my gal.

I learned my lesson that semester: as a director, never be desperate.

'Tis true in life too, isn't it?

Sometimes the fact that someone can walk and talk, and that they don't have moss growing between their teeth is all we look for in order to develop a friendship. And then, sadly sometimes, we even drop the requirement of no-moss. We're desperate. We assume that nobody likes us anyhow, and so we hang with whoever might let us stick around.

Yep, I've done the desperate dance. Yuck! Okay, here comes the humiliating scoop on it—proof that I love ya if I'm going to spill on myself just to help get a point across!

When I was twenty-something, I, along with the fam, set sail for Africa. Yes, Africa, the big, scary continent on the other side of the world. After reading one too many Christian-heroes-of-the-past books, I was determined to be a martyr-missionary gal for God. So I traded my Big Macs for fried beetles. Tossed aside the styles of the States for bush-wear (with the shirt on, of course.) I dumped out the sodas. Turned off the tube. Threw away the makeup. Washed my hair in egg yolks. And made a decision to only socialize with the Africans I had so humbly come to serve. Sure, just call me Amy Carmichael . . . the likeness is so close. Um, sorry, but not!

However, after a year and a half of my self-imposed, no-entertainment, beans and rice martyr routine, coupled with a lack of acceptance from the tribal people toward Western society and thinking (i.e., Americans; i.e., . . . me!), I admit, I was done. Empty. Bored. Lonely. Tired. Hungry.

Desperate.

It first showed up in my love for movies. I'm a huge movie buff. I've seen my once-favorite flick over a hundred times. But because of my determination to be a super-spiritual poor person serving overseas, I didn't allow our family to have any DVDs. Yes, I'm aware of the fact that I'm the mom and I could have changed that rule. But in search of an abased and unnatural service to God, I didn't. My personal VHS collection consisted of a pious, well-disciplined limitation of one "fun" movie. Oh joy! Believe me, I was a royal blast of a parent during those eighteen months, poor kids! But to put it mildly, after a year and a half of nothing, we all could have watched reruns of the *Andy Griffith Show* and then begged for more!

Desperate.

Now, before we go further, you have to understand something. You think you've got it hard where you are picking friends? Just come to the rural parts of Africa! If you're looking for anyone who knows anything about Americans or your own culture or Texas or baseball or Disneyland or McDonalds or MTV or DVDs, you can't be choosy. The choices are few, and the people come and go there about as quickly as Britney Spears throws together two weddings. You kind of take what you can get when you can get it, regardless of everything else . . . if you're desperate.

Which was me!

So when this certain family, who had lived in the States before, decided to befriend us, I didn't complain, at least not outwardly. Hey, they spoke English. Big plus. And they did let us watch their huge stack of DVDs. On a big screen, too!

Sure, I admit that there were telltale signs blaring all around us that this family might not exactly be what most consider . . . um, say stable, or healthy . . . like in relationships and all. Tip one was evident by others' past difficulties with them and the reality that after eight years in Africa they didn't have any friends.

But you're forgetting that I was desperate.

So I ignored the warning signs.

When you're desperate you take what you can get, right?

I did.

And, truth sadly be told, our family ended up experiencing a tremendous amount of pain from that relationship over the next months. We eventually ended it entirely, although it was too late to pull out totally unaffected.

And the lesson that was learned? Stash your own DVDs! (Actually, I'm kind of obsessed with getting movies at the moment, so if you're ever in the mood for watching something, just pop in. I probably own it!)

But seriously, the most important lesson learned: don't be desperate. It's not worth it. You end up willing to trade something good in yourself for something that will not satisfy you and that will probably harm you.

Being desperate as a director is bad, sure, but being desperate for a friend is dangerous.

Hear me out, here. When you think you're desperate, you lose all sense of reason and rationale. You give up a lot of who you are in exchange for something that you only think you need. We read in the Old Testament that a guy named Esau (the son of Isaac, the son of Abraham) was so desperate for food one day that he—you'll never believe this, it's so dumb—traded his entire inheritance—his birthright, his future, his security, and his honor—for a bowl of soup. I am sure the bowl of soup wasn't worth that price.

Don't be desperate! Learn ways to meet your legitimate needs. They might be ways you never dreamed of. But they need to be healthy ways, with boundaries.

Remember, if we have God, which we do, then He has promised to give us all we need to be satisfied. Sometimes we have to look for what He has given us and what He is providing. Sometimes we make ourselves desperate because we don't want to accept the relationships or the family or the activities we have, so we blow those and end up taking whatever else we can get. When we feel like we don't have all we need, then it's often because we're searching in the wrong alleys.

But if, from pain and circumstances, you forget that, and you get to thinking that you are desperate, **then please, please, please e-mail me (heather@kregel.com) or e-mail or call someone** who has a heart for teen girls. Talk to us. Tell us about your situation. Tell us the things that are happening that make you feel lonely, scared, and needy. You are never so desperate that you should allow someone else to use you, put you down, laugh at you, control you, manipulate you, or wound you. You don't need that. That's not a friend. **That's a leech.**

CHAPTER 10

BEING CHOOSY

You want to know what a real friend looks like?

You've got one.

Jesus.

Jesus is the only one who loves us with a love that is unconditional. He is the only one who accepts us in our entirety, without makeup, ten pounds heavier than what we want to be, and on a grumpy-gills sort of day.

There's no need to impress Him. Anyhow, we couldn't if we tried. No need to earn His acceptance. It's been paid for with a price. We don't have to dress up for Him. We don't have to carry our own books, even, when we stroll with Him, 'cause we trade our books, and our burdens, and our worries for a life of peace!

If you allow Him to, Jesus can be your very best friend. Now, don't think I'm lame. Listen up: He will never betray you. Never dis you. Never leave you. Never lie to you. Never reject you. Never hold back His love from you only to give you a cold and icy stare instead. He will never abandon you. He will never embarrass you for being who you are. Never use you.

He adores you. He loves you. He knows you. He accepts you. He even loves your one funky, guy-style pair of shoes. He loves you.

Yes, you.

While others may judge the way you dress, or the music you choose, or the abortion you had, or the language you use, or your eating and cutting habits, or your fears, or your impure thoughts, or your bossy tongue, or your obsession with having things under control, or your fears, Jesus knows all of these things about you and yet He loves you still.

Just like He loves me, too.

No, I didn't say that He loves the things that we do that inevitably hurt ourselves and others, but honestly, yes, He does love me and you.

He is our friend.

He is not fooled by an image or an attempt you might make at being a super good Christian on the outside, either. He certainly wasn't fooled by my great missionary sacrifices! He was more interested in my heart. He knows our hearts and our selfish little thoughts. And what's better, He accepts us in spite of them all. God knows we've all suffered hurts that often show up in actions we later regret.

You can't shock Christ. He won't run away screaming in disbelief. In fact, you can't even push Him away. Sure, discipline or loving correction from Him may come when we make bad decisions, but for a heart who humbly cries out to Him, no matter what, no matter when, no matter where . . . He's there.

There was a famous Hollywood actor named Rock Hudson who died some time ago of AIDS. During his day, homosexuality was not as openly talked about as it is now. So he hid his lifestyle. He was gay. He had a partner. Actually, he had a few. He tried to cover his hurts, disappointments, and betrayals in life in this particular way.

Someone wrote that on Rock's deathbed, he sought a man of the faith to lead him through confessing his rebellions and sins, and he begged for God's mercy.

Do you think God gave it?

The answer to that question is nailed to a cross. You bet He did! Just like He gives His mercy to us.

God is our friend with a love that is unconditional.

He is your friend.

And mine, too.

We can trust Him.

His heart breaks over the betrayal you experienced as a small child. He shudders at your parents' divorce. He weeps when He sees you were left so many times in the care of those who might not have cared so much for you. He hears the names you were called in elementary school. He knows if you were raised in an angry home. He knows the shame you willingly wear even though it's not your own. He bears the scars of each and every move you were made to do. He feels your broken arm. Or the obsession with your weight. Or your poverty. Or your wealth. Or your disease. He knows your pain. He knows your loneliness. He knows your hate.

And He invites you to trust Him with all of that, as your friend. He wants you to give it all to Him, as a friend who offers you peace and acceptance in exchange for doubt and rejection.

He accepts you.

As is.

Because He loves you.

He loves you, girl. Yes, you. And me. With all of our foibles (isn't that a fun word?). He really does.

His friendship is a true friendship. And if you have Him, then you're not desperate. Not at all.

It's only that we sometimes forget that, don't we? I have, unfortunately. But He is still there . . . will always be there . . . until we never forget again. And because of Him, and what He says about us, we are worth having real friends.

You are worth having true friends. You are worth friends who respect you. Who honor you. Who don't use you. Who encourage you.

And they are out there. Loads of them. You just need to let them know that you are out there too. And by letting them know, I'm not talking about shooting out a desperate little memo like I did for my play and then accepting whoever shows up.

Nope.

If a director puts out a memo that reads: Needed: players. Not sure what the title of the play is. Not sure when the script will be done. Don't know if we have a venue yet. Can't guarantee payment. Call me, please, because I don't have the guts to call you—who's going to turn up? Those who can't land a better gig, that's who. And if someone can't land a better gig than one made in a cry of desperation, there is usually a reason why.

But if the director bills her play as one with imagination, creativity, promise, and poise, she's going to get a lot more qualified and trained gals and guys from whom to make her choice.

Same thing with friends.

Have you, by chance, been drawing those who are not so faithful, loyal, kind, or true? Could it be that the problem lies in the memos you send out? Remember the 93 percent? The way you carry yourself. What you wear or don't wear. The way you walk. Shoulders shrugged and drooping. Sad eyes. Head down. And don't forget the 7 percent, too, the way you talk. Short or shallow conversations. Jabs at others. Jabs at yourself. Control patterns and bossy tendencies. Or could it be that you have a lack of confidence and you feel you don't deserve good friends?

Ah . . . but you do.

You do deserve it.

A cast of great friends begins with you.

This is your play.

This is your life.

This is your story.

You're not a victim in a poorly written plotline.

Rather, you are the director of a really cool script. A script with *you* as the title!

And since you're a director, it's high time for some tips on directing.

There's this movie that I really love about this dead guy named Amadeus. Okay, so he's not really all that dead in the movie (that would be gross . . . and weird!), he's just dead now and—don't worry—he's safely buried away.

Short history blurb (I promise this won't take long): Wolfgang Amadeus Mozart was a piano player and a composer a long time ago in a galaxy far, far away. Well, maybe it wasn't a galaxy far, far away, but he did live in a different country on another continent, and he spoke a language that sounds more like he was coughing out some broccoli stuck in his throat rather than that he was actually talking, which makes it seem like another galaxy, for sure. And so a movie was made about him. End of history blurb. Pretty painless, right?

When the movie *Amadeus* came out, though, it won a jumble of awards for all sorts of things, including an Academy Award for the very best picture of the year. Now that's some big air! Whoever directed *Amadeus* probably knows a tad about directing, wouldn't you say? Tune in. This is what the director said, "A good director—always, for every part of his work—must choose people who are better than him."[1]

Did you catch that? "A good director . . . must choose people who are *better* than him."

Ah! Doesn't that sound a bit risky, though? I mean, if we hang with people who are better than us, then doesn't that mean they aren't going to like us? They aren't going to look up to us? What will keep them around?

Hmmm . . . I don't know, maybe . . . say, you?

Hard to believe?

Shouldn't be. 'Tis true.

What if a friend of yours is better at how she chooses her clothes and puts them together? And you let her know this. Or what if another friend is better at you in math? And you don't make her feel weird about it. And another friend is better at soccer, a game you know you could never understand. And another friend is better at being kind to people who are usually ignored.

Snaps for them!

What if all of these friends liked hanging around you because they can tell you aren't jealous or intimidated by them? You're cool enough already with who you are. And you even encourage them by what you say and do? Don't you think that in time those strong parts in their lives might actually rub off on you and make you a more rounded person? No. I don't mean more rounded in the rear end and thighs! I mean more rounded in that you get a bit better at coordinating your clothes, doing your math, understanding soccer, or being nice to people who are usually ignored. By watching your friends succeed in their areas and by not just chucking them and being jealous of or intimidated by them, you—as a group of friends—will all be better as a result.

We've got a lot we can learn from others.

Why not try?

I don't mean that you're going to surround yourself with only those people who are so much better than you in all areas. A good director doesn't surround herself with better directors. She surrounds herself with those people who do well in what she can't do. Like lighting. Filming. Acting. Costuming. And other things.

You're still the director. You're still in charge of you.

But in friendships, we need friends who are better than us in things too. We need to learn from them. And grow. We need to stop being jealous of each other and benefit, instead, as a whole.

I think the best example of this happened at an awards ceremony for the movie *The Lord of the Rings: Return of the King.* Now, I totally apologize if you're not a huge Frodo fan, but this is a rock of an example, so hang for a while.

Your personal opinion aside, *LOTR: Return of the King* is considered a great film and a major accomplishment. It got eleven Academy

Awards for stuff like Best Picture, Best Score, Best Special Effects . . . and loads of other stuff. The *Return of the King* won in every category for which it was nominated. No other film, ever, pulled down so many tricks in one turn. The thrilled cast and crew got to celebrate and celebrate and celebrate time and time again.

But the funny thing is that no one, not even one single actor (no, not even cutie Orlando Bloom), got so much as a nomination for an acting job.

None.

I guess it's not all that funny, though. More like it's to be expected. Especially in light of the fact that on another night in another arena, the entire LOTR cast won the SAG (Screen Actors Guild) award for Best Ensemble Cast in a Film. That means they got the award for the best GROUP of actors who performed well together as a WHOLE.

After all, that's how acting is supposed to work. You pull together. You lean on each other. Because if someone shines too much, then someone else has to suffer in her shadow—darkening the overall result. The best pics come, however, when the group of players plays well together.

Friends. It's more than Jennifer Aniston. She couldn't have made that show alone.

The same holds true in life.

The same holds true in friendships.

The same holds true with each other.

Gee, I wonder if God knew that when He gave us the script for loving one another as much as we love ourselves?

Bet so.

And on awards night in that distant day when the return of the True King is at hand, I hope that we can look up and hear Him say that we really did learn how to play—and play well—together.

And, as a result, we will all jump up and down and get to celebrate and celebrate and celebrate, again and again.

Sounds like a party I don't want to miss.

How 'bout you?

CHAPTER 11

ROLE CALL!

Know something? I'm going to give you the naked truth on girl-friends right now. No sugar coating. No allegiance to tact. Why? Because I'm tired of seeing what we do to each other as girls.

I got a reminder of this the other night when my daughter Tayte and I sat down to catch a few minutes on the tube together. It was a British reality TV program about these teens who sign up for a couple of months of living in the jungle. Fun show. It kind of follows their relationships and struggles while they're out there.

But the thing that got me, which wasn't so fun, happened between these two teen girls. They had been assigned as buddies. Quick description:

Girl One—we'll call her "**Blondie**"—was blonde, cute, bubbly, smart, fun, and scored high in the areas most teen girls worry about such as looks, body, and blah, blah, blah.

Girl Two—ah, let's call her "**Red**"—was a redhead, needed braces, was smart, quiet, and self-described as "melancholy." Yeah, Red pretty much struggled in all those areas that teen girls worry about such as looks, body, and blah, blah, blah again.

Well, **Blondie** and **Red** were assigned to each other as buds. This meant they were to live together, work together, and watch out for each other. But all **Red** could do, at first, was complain about her partner. She complained on camera. She cried. She didn't want to be paired up with **Blondie**. She put **Blondie** down, made fun of her, and was not friendly to her at all.

So . . . yep, **Blondie** got her feelings hurt. You bet. She wasn't sure what she had done to give Red such a pill. But she knew that **Red** didn't like her, for some reason.

Good for **Blondie**, though, that she was mature enough to go to the camp counselors early on and bring everything out in the open for a chit and a chatter. Because in that chat she found out that **Red** really did like her. **Red** just acted like she didn't because she thought **Blondie** was so much better than she was and so obviously wouldn't like anyone as unworthy as her.

Once the air was cleared, though, they were able to be good buds.

Too bad we live in such a fog sometimes instead of the jungle, isn't it? It's a rare case when the air gets cleared. Instead, people's feelings just end up getting hurt and certain girls, most often the ones the world considers pretty or cool, end up without many real friends at all. That's cuz everyone else is too scared of them.

There's a counselor in Christian teen ministry, Soul Sista, who has worked directly with teens for nearly a decade. She recently told me about some confessions made to her around the campfires of ministry. Christian teens told her that they didn't like to be friends with girls who were prettier than them. They found it easier to pick friends who were heavier or not as pretty, because, they said, that way when you are with her, you can feel better about yourself.

Makes sense, sure, and it's not a bad plan for pumping the self-image some. It's just that when was the purpose of friendships to boost your own self-esteem? That's not a friend, that's an agent. Hire one.

There's a huge group of Blondies out there in this world who get the cold shoulder, the gossip, and the general rejection of many of their peers simply because they are pretty. Come on, girls. Blondies have just as many feelings as everyone else. And they need friends, too.

Ever heard the saying, "Don't hate me because I'm beautiful"? It'd be good if that saying didn't hold true in Christian camps, but it does. So on behalf of the Blondies in the body of Christ, I'm saying it for them: don't hate them because they're beautiful!

Our acceptance and security can't come from what we wear or how we look or who we hang with. It comes from Christ. And when we understand that, then Blondies won't threaten us.

So not only do we need to step it up and overcome jealousy and insecurity in order to hang with great pals, we also need to look for friends who are just plain good at being loyal, honest, humble, kind, fun, and unique. Sure, it's doubtful we're going to find a friend who is great at all those things rolled up in one. More likely, we're going to find friends who are extra good at being wise, or extra good at being fun, or extra good at being tight and true.

Those are the gals we need to hang with and script into our play.

I've put together a little list—like a casting call of sorts—roles to look for and fill, or avoid, in the stories of our lives. We've got two categories here: the girls to "go with" through life, and the girls to "go without." Let's skim through, okay?

The Go-With Girls! Girls to Go with in Finding and Developing Friendships

Go-To Girl

Every gal needs a go-to girl. This is someone you can go to when things get tough. This is the girl who is humble and wise and has a love for God and His truth. She might even be a bit older than you. She's a friend to have when you need advice. Okay, for me, that's often! Like . . . daily!

The go-to girl has proven herself by setting you straight in the past. She'd make a good counselor some day. She doesn't talk and tell. She understands the sticky parts of life. She's a good listener, is slow to judge, and quick to offer direction in the middle of a puddle of mud.

It's really great if you can identify and have a go-to girl in your life. It's also great if you can reach out and be that go-to girl to someone who might be a bit younger than you, too! We can all do that for someone who needs us!

It's good to test the waters first, though, as you seek out this person, kind of like what a director in a screen test might do. Maybe you ought not dump the whole wagon on someone at first but just give her a little bit of the dirt you might be dealing with at the moment. If you later hear about it through another friend or find it scrawled on the bathroom walls, well, that might be a clue that the girl you sought out isn't a true go-to girl at all. A true go-to girl will keep it private, out of respect for you.

Go-Go Girl

The go-go girl is the one who makes you giggle! She seems to be always on the go. She always has an idea of things to do that are fun. She brightens a room with her smile. She cheers you up when you're feeling blue . . . or green . . . or even purple.

Everybody benefits from a go-go girl in her life. Somebody to remind them that the thing that's bothering them will pass and there are good things to be found right now.

You can pick out a go-go girl by her face. The cheer in her eyes. The way she looks at life with hope and joy and a bit of a sparkle. You got a bum grade in biology? She'll have you joking and laughing in no time and believing that you can do better on the next try. Your jeans accentuate what they shouldn't? She'll convince you that you're starting a new trend and then persuade you to celebrate by sharing a fat-free ice cream!

A true go-go girl will know her boundaries, though, and understand that real fun comes when lines of safety and respect for others are honored. You'll feel secure around her. Free, yet still safe and fun.

Go-Through-It Girl

This is your yellow lab of friendships. The girl who will stick by you come what may. We all crave that loyal relationship in our life. It's hard to find it but it's there. A go-through-it girl will go through the struggles and questions in life with you and not abandon you when things get tough.

She's the girl you can sit with while you're waiting for your ride or for the bus, and you can run out of things to say. And she's okay with it. You don't have to entertain her.

How can you find this girl? Well, she might not be a go-go girl and a go-to girl rolled into one. Her strength is her loyalty. You'll see it when others walk away. Or when someone in school doesn't have many friends and she still manages to smile at them and find a way to brighten their day. She's confident enough in herself and in the God who loves her that she doesn't need to keep switching over to who might be the "hot" spot at the moment.

Look for her. She probably won't be in the limelight. But you can spot her, nonetheless. And when you find her, you'll be glad you did.

Just like a play or a movie is made up of a cast of many, so should your life. One person can't be a go-to, a go-go, and a go-through-it tootsie roll for you. That's not fair to ask of her. It takes a cast and crew of many to make a story chime. Everyone has diverse strengths. Life is about combining, joining, teamwork, and being stronger, because the whole is greater than the parts.

We need good friends. And there are more different kinds of friends to have than just the three we've jotted down. But I wanted to save some space for the kinds of friends that we would do best to avoid as well. The friends that aren't really friends at all. The ones that we could go-without.

Remember—this is your play. Your life. Your script. You wouldn't want to cast Barney, the big purple dinosaur, in a leading role, would you? Neither should you cast girls who, for some reason or another, have also not yet learned how to grow.

But that's not kind to them, you say? Shouldn't we love everyone?

Love, yes.

But sometimes love means not helping, or enabling, someone to continue in a destructive pattern of behavior or thinking. And your open friendship might just enable that for a time. I'm not saying to be mean to these gals and put them down. I'm just saying they're probably not yet ready for a part in your inner-clan.

Let's look at who these gals might be:

The Go-Without Girls! Girls to Go Without When Finding and Developing Friendships

Go-Around Girl

This is the girl who will go-around you telling all sorts of things that you confided in her or that she saw you do. Another word for that? Gossip.

One cue to uncovering go-around girls is if they gossip about other people to you. "Did you hear what Kelly did the other day?" or "You really need to pray for Mandy because she's going through this really tough time right now . . . let me tell you about it," or "I can trust you right? This is just between me and you, but Trent and Trish got it on after youth group the other night in the basement storage room."

Listen up. If she's talking about other people like that, she's going to talk about you too. The go-around girl lives for spreading bad news, maybe because it makes her feel more important or more powerful, who knows. But you're not going to cure her or change her by being her close friend. You're going to enable her to continue.

The best thing to do is to confront her in a loving way and tell her that it's not a good thing to talk about other people like that.

Remind her that nobody ever really knows the heart behind a matter, only God, and He's made it clear that we shouldn't judge or spread gossip.

Still be nice to her. But she's not going to cut it as a true friend.

Go-On Girl

The go-on girl does exactly that. She's a cousin to the pink Energizer bunny and goes on and on and on and on and on and on and . . . Did I mention that she goes on? She's obsessed with herself and goes on about her achievements and successes or, as she puts it, all the stresses in her life.

She comes up for air every once in a while but then she dives back in. It's all about her. *Her* struggles. *Her* dreams. *Her* hopes. *Her* failures. *Her* zits. *Her* hair. *Her* shoes. *Her* jeans. *Her* parents. *Her* boyfriend. *Her* room. *Her* iPod. *Her* job.

Okay. You get the point.

It's all about her.

Now, true, each of us needs someone to talk to about ourselves at some point or another. That's communicating. Sharing. Being open, honest, and all that jazz. But there needs to be a definite give and take kind of thing going on in real relationships.

If you've just sat through an hour soap on your friend's life and you try to nudge in with two minutes about something that happened to you and your dog, Shell, and she brings it all back to herself and her dog, Bark, well, chances are she's not thinking about anyone else but her number one gal . . . herself.

That's not friendship.

Friendship happens between two people who can share and care and laugh together. What you've got with the go-on girl is the equivalent of an old-fashioned radio show. She's the radio. You're sitting in the rocking chair knitting away. Slippers anyone?

Go-on girls are a bit self-centered, for whatever reasons. Rather than just dumping her and not helping her to discover why her friends keep running away, you might want to gently fill her in that her focus seems to be a bit one-sided.

That's the loving thing to do, at least if you do it with a loving heart and not with a jab to hurt her. You're helping her to see that selfishness doesn't really satisfy at all. The quicker she sees that, the better chance she has at becoming and keeping great friends in the end.

Go-Up Girl

What exactly is a go-up girl? She's someone who likes to plot her way on the backs of others. She likes to climb the ladders. She doesn't believe she has what it takes to get there on her own, so she uses people.

She will try to dominate your time. She will try to control your schedule. She'll make you feel bad if for some reason you didn't sit with her at lunch. She needs you, because she has a plan. She'll do anything until she's gotten where she wants to be through you. Then she'll drop you.

A go-up girl changes friends frequently. At first you might be flattered when she talks nice to you and tells you what you want to hear and pays so much attention to you. But a go-up girl only gives what she thinks will bring a return. That's not a true friend and your heart is better off investing itself in friends who really care about you for who you are and not for what they can get from you.

How to tell a go-up girl from a true friend? Let her down once, gently. Maybe tell her that you can't join her shopping, or at the movies, or that you can't sit with her at lunch. And see how she responds. If she tries to make you feel guilty with a sigh or some unkind words said with a smile, then that's a sign that her friendship isn't a friendship. It's a rope.

Let her go. You are worth more.

So there you have it, a small start toward discovering and landing a great cast of friends in your life. You are worth surrounding yourself with friends who are faithful, fun, and true. You can attract them by having the same qualities yourself. Are you a go-to girl? A go-go girl? Or a go-through-it girl? Where does your strength lie and what do you have to offer your friendships? Grow that. Go with it. You'll be glad you did, because we need friends. We all do.

We can't make it on our own. We weren't designed to.

It's like this true story I read once about an airplane that this man was fixing, and for some reason he left the plane running with the throttle up while he was working on it. So when he was testing the propellers, the plane started rolling. And there it went without him, faster and faster down the runway.

Since the throttle had been left up, guess what? Right-o, the plane took off.

On its own.

Alone.

There was nobody with whom to share the ride.

A few hours after the plane took off, you got it, it crashed. It ran out of gas. In the air. And it tumbled. Because it was flying alone.

You see, an empty plane just isn't able to land itself safely and fuel up for another time.[1]

Same with me.

Same with you.

I need friends.

You need friends, too.

True friends.

Good friends. Friends to laugh with, chat with, cry with, and know.

Friends forever.

Friends for the now.

Friends.

Real friends.

Your own cast of friends . . . starring in your own play.

CHAPTER 12

GUY TALK

I'm sitting at a coffee shop punching out the last pages of this book. I've got my laptop on the table in front of me. A song by the Eagles blasts in the background—or is that Constantine Maroulis? Can't tell anymore.

The room is filled with people as diverse as the tunes I've downloaded on my Mac. Some are friends. Others . . . maybe not.

A man from India talks things over with an African-American guy in the corner across from me. The man from India's glasses rest near the end of his nose. He listens, a bit skeptically it seems with his arms crossed and his legs crossed, kind of like a ready-to-eat pretzel. I think the other guy is trying to sell him something because he moves his arms a lot. Smiles a lot. The man from India offers a strained laugh.

A husband and wife sit across from me, her head rests on the edge of his overstuffed yellow chair. He fiddles with a laptop. She reaches for her smoothie. It's empty. She goes to the counter and gets another one. I think they're Japanese. Her hair hangs straight as silk. She's pretty.

Some blond-haired, blue-eyed silver-spooners pour themselves into a couple of medical books in the corner beside me. One of them broke the mold and has a tattoo on his left arm. He's in a tight T. The other one shakes his foot on the table—whether he does so out of nervousness or boredom, I don't know. Surely researching ligaments, tendons, and all those blood cells must be enthralling.

Two women old enough to be my grandmoms walk past me toward the bathroom. They're wearing pink from head to toe. One has black polka dots on her pink. Reminds me of something I wore in the eighth grade.

I'm in Dallas. I like Dallas. I like the diversity in the play being scripted right before me. Different skin colors. Hair colors. Accents. Faces. Clothes. Smiles. Frowns. All of it. I like it. Makes things interesting . . . unlike the framed art hanging on the wall straight in front of me.

I don't know why but this coffee shop owner-guy put the same picture up one, two, three, four, five—no, six times. Yep. The exact same one. Maybe he's trying to sell them. "Would you like a picture today with your latte?"

Um, no thanks. I'll pass.

But I don't get it. There they are. Six paintings of the same bird. Blue head. Green shoulder. Red belly and purple wings.

The same bird. Six times. The same eye. Same beak. Same frame.

Boring.

I stare at the birds. But only for a moment. My eyes return instead to the array of diversity around me. And I smile. Forget the birds. Life is too short for boring. But we're boring sometimes, aren't we? We surround ourselves with the same people. The same styles. The same lingo. The same dreams. Even the same sex. We forget that there's a world out there waiting to sparkle up our one-gal show. We just need to see it.

But we so often don't. Because diversity sometimes scares us. And understandably so. There's a big professional word for this fear: xenophobia. It's a dislike and fear of things, people, ways that are foreign to us. It's a fear of the unknown. And that fear is legitimate, to a degree. It's like me taking one of my hubby's African bush-pastors who has never so much as ridden in a car and dropping him here in the States on a loopy-loop roller coaster. The man would freak. He wouldn't know that when he goes upside down that the buckles would hold him and that the ride is safe. He would think that I just sent him to his death.

Or if I were to take you and drop you in Africa, pretty much alone after dark in the middle of nowhere at a Maasai manyatta (a round circle of mud huts) with hyenas, giraffe, and lions outside the circle and twenty-something Moran Maasai's at the entrance of the circle all jumping up and down and chanting with spears in their hands . . . looking fierce. You would freak . . . kind of like I did, even though I did my best to be polite, hide the freak-face, and smile instead as I walked past the guys. But I freaked inside because I didn't know if these guys were going to shish kebab me or what!

It was only in time that I learned that the Maasai are really cool people who wouldn't harm a stranger unless you messed with their cows. And I hadn't. But until I knew that, I was vulnerable. A Maasai kid standing next to me in the dark asked B for his watch. "Give him your watch!" I whispered. "Quickly—give it to him!" I nearly yanked the thing off B's wrist.

Yet if I were in the same situation today the kid could forget the watch altogether! In fact, I would give him a few words on how impolite it is to ask for someone's property right off their body.

We make mistakes when fear and ignorance guide us. We give into things that ultimately harm us. A guy says you need to kiss him to prove that you love him. And we do it. But the only thing we've proved is that we're stupid and we have no idea who guys are, how to love them or even what love is. After all, you had thought the two of you were only "good friends."

Come on girls, we need to learn about the people that don't come from our own type of background. We need to learn what their expectations are and how they communicate and what things mean to them. Because the real stuff we've been talking about doesn't always mean the same thing to others as what it means to us.

Being friends with guys can be great fun. But it can also be great pain because we're different. If we assume that they're like us and treat them the way we treat our gals, we're going to flop. Big time. And someone is going to get hurt.

So let's keep in mind that we're dealing with a different species here. Sure, they might speak the same language, and eat with their mouths, and walk on two feet, but guys are different. And far be it from me to be the one to talk about how friendships with guys would work best. I'm in your boat on this one. So rather, I've asked Brian and Henry to come along and give us some pointers on their kind. B and Uncle H are going to tell us some things about guys and how to have friendships with them so that we can do it well. So that we won't end up getting played. Nor will we break any hearts of our own.

You in? You ready for some tips on how to have better relationships with the boys? Grab them—the tips, not the boys—cuz it's all about love, and love means knowing how to live, laugh, and learn together.

Order a latte. Forget the framed art. Grab a chair. This should be good.

GUY TALK 1: HENRY

When I was a teen, back in the 1970s when polyester shirts and platform shoes were in, I had no idea that girls ever thought about guys. I knew we could be amusing and cute at times, but I never thought girls spent a lot of time or energy thinking about us. After all, we could be gross, insensitive, and sometimes we didn't even smell too good. What girl would ever want to think about us? Well, I was wrong. Having three daughters has taught me a lot about teenage girls. And one thing I have learned from them is that you girls think and talk about guys . . . a lot.

Over the past eight years I have had the joy and burden of coaching my daughters on the male gender: what to look for, who to avoid, how to talk to them, how to dress. We've covered all the do's and don'ts . . . more than once. The reason is simple. I love my daughters.

You may be asking yourself why my daughters would ever want to listen to an old guy like me. That's another simple answer. My daughters know three very important things:

1. No man on planet earth loves them as much as I do.

2. God has given **me** the responsibility of being their father, and it's a responsibility that I take very seriously.

3. By God's grace, I have been successful in life. Not perfect by any means, but God has given me wisdom that they could certainly benefit from.

In their eyes, that list makes me very valuable as they grow and mature.

So, yes, I know a lot about guys. I know there are guys with great character and I also know there are goofballs. Every school and neighborhood has both. Years ago, Mark Twain wrote a book that became a classic titled, **The Prince and the Pauper.** Well, I'd like to talk to you about the prince and the pretender. Sadly, the pretender can look a lot like the prince. When you kiss a pretender, he won't turn into a frog, but he will slowly steal your hopes and dreams.

So ladies, will you grant me the privilege of coaching you a bit on guys? I am one, I am raising one, and I care very much about how guys treat girls. Let's begin by giving you a few guys to avoid. Some of you have not been tangled up with these guys yet. That's great news! When you meet them you'll know them . . . and you'll know to stay away. Of course, when some of you read this list, the names of certain boys may pop into your mind. You might even be dating one of these guys now!

GUYS TO AVOID

Sassy Son

This is the guy who treats his mother poorly. If a son is disrespectful to his mother, why in the world would you ever think that he would treat you any different? Listen to him talk to and about his mother. Is he respectful? Does he honor her? Does he help her? If the answer to these questions is no, it's time to say so long to the sassy son.

Dishonest Dude

This is the guy who lies, cheats, steals, or sometimes all three! Does he cheat at school? Does he lie to others? Here we go again, if he lies to others, he will most certainly lie to you. If you catch a guy like this, it's time to discard the dishonest dude.

Locker-room Lecturer

At times guys can be crude and vulgar. For years this dialog has been referred to as "locker-room" conversation. It's how guys may talk around other guys. Yes, that's bad enough, but unfortunately, some guys have no problem talking crass around girls. Girls send a loud and horrible message when they condone that conversation or even participate in it. The message they send is that it's okay. Girls, it's not okay for guys to talk crass or vulgar around a princess, and that's exactly who you are if you have put your trust in Christ. You are a daughter of the King! It is okay for you to say, "I don't like it when you talk that way." Comments like that set you apart as a young woman of excellence. So if the locker-room lecturer ever opens his mouth around you, send him to the gutter.

Girl Gazer

This guy has no trouble looking at other girls, even if you are watching him. He stares and mentally undresses them. His lust does not sleep and the day will come when he will verbally compare you to someone else. Get away from the girl gazer. He will slowly chip away at your self-esteem and make you feel inadequate. His comments will be a sharp contrast to the King who says you are "fearfully and wonderfully made."

Lecherous Lucky

This poor sap has three things on his mind: sex, sex, and sex. He's looking to score. Singles and doubles don't interest him. He wants to round third and make it home. He even uses sappy lines like, "If you love me you'll let me" or "This will prove that we love each other." He won't care about you. Like Tamar's half-brother Amnon in 2 Samuel 13, he'll hate you once he's had you. My heart breaks for girls who give themselves sexually to a guy knowing "he's the one," only to be dumped by him later. When Lecherous Lucky throws you a line, tell him he's fishing in the wrong pond.

In the chorus of an old Backstreet Boys song they told teen girls that if they wanted to be a good girl, they would need to find a bad boy. Maybe a boy like one of those I just mentioned. With songs like that, it's no wonder that they were on the back street. Just keep them off your street. Girls, if you ever get advice like that, whoever gives it to you has just been disqualified from being an influence in your life.

Good girls certainly don't need bad boys and for that matter, bad girls don't need bad boys. If you find one it's time to flee. What good girls need are young men with great character.

My son Henry is one of those guys. He has more character at sixteen than I did at thirty. My son is my hero because he is becoming the young man I wish I had been. Let me give you one example. When he was twelve years old he spent the night at a friend's house with two other guys and one of the boys put in a pornographic DVD for them to watch. What did my son do? He came home and told me about it. The others called him chicken, and he told them he was a Christian. His walk matches his talk, and he's not confusing as he lives his life. And you ought to see how he treats his mother! My wife has always felt blessed to have such a loving son who honors her.

Yes, I know firsthand that teen guys with character are out there, but you have to look closely.

Guys to Find

Well, we've looked at the pretenders, so how can you identify the prince? The prince is the guy you can trust. He's a guy who has a bold walk with Christ. He's the one who cares for you and has your best interests in mind. And yes, he's the guy that could one day be your husband. Indeed, he's the tall tree in the forest.

You can't find him by **looking** at guys, but you can find him by **watching** them. Looking and watching? Yup . . . there is a huge difference between the two. If you simply look at a guy, you will notice things like the style of clothes he wears, his extra-curricular activities, or even the scent of cologne he puts on. But there is so much more you need to know. Watch him. Watch how he acts in class. Watch how he treats his friends and other girls. Watch how he walks his talk. Does he live his life mindful of his commitment to Christ, or is he confusing?

Do you know what you want your future husband to be like? I bet you do. That's another thing I've learned from my daughters—you ladies love to think about what you hope he's like. I bet many of you even have a list in your mind. What's on it? I've got a few qualities that need to be on your list if you are looking for the prince.

I didn't come up with the list myself. I first saw it in the book of Galatians: "But the fruit of the Spirit is love, joy, peace, patience, kindness, goodness, faithfulness, gentleness, self-control; against such things there is no law" (Gal. 5:22–23 NASB).

Pretty neat list, don't you think? I think it's worth our time to look at each item on the list. After all, these are the qualities of your prince!

Love

Does he love God, his family, and others at school? One of the greatest compliments I think we could ever hear is, "I've never heard you say a bad word about anybody." If he has love, he doesn't have bad words to say about others. He's too busy looking for ways to express his love for others.

Joy

I love the joy the apostle Paul expresses in his prison epistles. Yes, he wrote them from prison. For Paul, his joy was dependent on his relationship with Christ, not his circumstances. For teenagers, it's easy today to find trials to worry about, but your prince will demonstrate joy in the midst of them. How would you expect a guy to respond if his team lost the big game? I've been to high school football games where I saw players stomp off the field throwing their helmet and kicking their feet. Ahh, but the prince is the first one to walk across the field to shake an opposing player's hand for a well-played game. Why? Because his happiness does not depend on his happenings. In the midst of failure and disappointment he has joy that comes from God. So if the prince loses a game, fails a test, or can't find a job, he won't dwell on the problem. He's busy looking for possibilities.

Peace

Every day in pubic school my kids see fighting of some kind. Maybe it's a fistfight in the cafeteria or maybe it's two friends who are not talking to each other. Well, your prince will be a man of peace. He's a peacemaker who is impacting others. Two words the peacemaker has in his vocabulary are, "I'm sorry." Ladies, if you have a relationship with a guy who does not apologize, but always waits for you to say those two wonderful words, then I doubt he is a peacemaker. The prince knows how to say "I'm sorry" and will do so when he is wrong to mend the relationship. That's impacting!

Patience

It is so easy to be impatient today. We have lines at the mall, on highways, and even in fast food restaurants. How are we supposed to respond to lines? I know how your prince will respond. He'll be patient. He knows that girls take longer to get ready. He knows they take longer in the bathroom. The prince won't rush you; instead he'll wait for you . . . patiently. We'll address self-control in a second, but he also won't pressure you to do something sexually. The prince has patience to wait for God's timing.

Kindness

One of my favorite verses is Micah 6:8. It tells us that the Lord loves kindness. The pretender will be kind to his friends. The prince will be kind to everyone. Do you have cliques in your school? Sure you do. Every school has them. Someone in a clique associates with others in the group and has little to say to anyone else. Not so with the prince. Watch him around students who are not cool or popular. His kindness makes others feel important.

Goodness

It's so sad to me that being labeled "good" is derogatory in many schools. I remember once when my daughter Whitney was mocked for being a "good girl." The pretender will shy away from that label and the prince will wear it like a badge of honor knowing that his goodness is a mark of his faith. As you examine guys, ask yourself this question, "Would teachers fight to have a classroom full of students like him?" If the answer is yes, he has the makings of a prince because his behavior honors God.

Faithfulness

When I get a chance to talk to the guys that my daughters date, we always talk about their faith in Christ. Take a look at the guys you spend time with, how are they doing in their walk? Do they attend church regularly? Are they plugged into a solid youth group at school or their church? When you spend time together, does your relationship with Christ come up in the conversation? Trust me, the prince will talk about Christ a lot because he has a growing faith.

Gentleness

A term we don't hear much today is "gentleman." The prince is gentle in words and deeds. Now what does that mean? Does that mean he is dainty or feminine? Nope . . . he's all man. A man's man is not a boisterous braggart who puts others down. He is a gentleman. His gentle words speak kindness and understanding. His gentle deeds are helpful to others. Don't be deceived into thinking he is weak. On the contrary, he is a man of great strength and character.

I have taught my son how to date. He has not been on a date yet, but he's ready. He knows how to talk respectfully to girls, and he knows how to open the door for a young lady. Oh yes, she will be safe in his company because the only agenda he will have is to honor God as he enjoys the company of a princess. And so it is with the prince. He will treat the princess like she is precious crystal. Find the prince, ladies, and you have found a gentleman.

Self-Control

This quality is vitally important as you discern the prince from the pretender. The prince demonstrates self-control; the pretender is selfish. If you date him, the prince will treat you the way he wants some guy to one day treat his own daughter. He does not want to see how far he can get with you. He wants to honor God as he dates you. So how do you see self-control in a guy if you are not dating? If he has self-control, you won't see him in a fight. You won't see him cheat. You won't see him say things to others that he later regrets. The prince knows how to keep his tongue and wits about him.

So that's our list to identify the prince. He wouldn't be the prince, however, unless he desired the same qualities in the princess. This is a good time to examine your heart. How do you do in each of these areas? To help you look at a couple of qualities, let's use the telephone. No, I don't want you to call anyone, but the telephone can help you see how much patience and self-control you display.

Telephone Conversation

One of the things I've learned as a father of teenage girls is that you ladies like the telephone. No, I should say you *love* the telephone. Well, let's look at a couple of phone tips when talking to guys.

PHONE TIP 1

Don't call guys on the telephone (patience and self-control). Make them call you. Guys are hunters and they love the pursuit. If girls appear to be too available, they'll send the wrong message. Please understand, I don't like it when girls play games with guys, but I think it's good for girls to be a bit mysterious. There is no mystery in calling a guy. He'll know you like him and can't wait to talk to him. And he may wonder, what else will you do to win his affection? Be patient, ladies, and let him call you.

PHONE TIP 2

When the guy does call, always end the conversation with him wanting to talk to you more (self-control). As Heather has said, guys and girls are different. Girls can talk to a guy for two hours on the phone and say, "Oh, that was a great conversation." Guys will be on the phone for two hours and say, "Wow, what a beating." This may be hard, but I recommend staying on the phone with a guy for no more than twenty to thirty minutes. That's it. After that much time, tell him you need to wash your hair or something and then go wash your hair. When you hang up he'll wish you would have stayed longer and the pursuit will be on because he'll see that he lost out to hair washing. He won't take you for granted. I'll probably get kicked out of the guy club for telling you that, but guys need to know that you are not available anytime they want you to be. The prince will pursue the princess. The pretender will lose interest and look for easier prey.

Pretty simple, huh? No games, no strategy to catch a guy, just helpful tips to discern the prince from the pretender so you can be safe until the right guy comes along. As you look at the list, you won't find a guy who does all of these things perfectly. But do you see solid evidence that he enjoys the fruit of the Spirit? These qualities will define him.

The good news is that God gives you discernment to find the prince in a culture filled with pretenders. When my daughter Whitney goes out with guys, I hug her and say three simple words, "Above all else." She will complete the proverb of Solomon with, "Guard your heart for it is the wellspring of life." You see, she dates with discernment and makes her boundaries clear. Why? She's waiting for the prince.

Now what about you? If I could sit across from you right now, I would coach you and encourage you to guard your heart and wait for the prince. One day you'll see firsthand that he's well worth the wait. And so are you, princess.

GUY TALK 2: BRIAN

You know girls, I feel for you. I mean, you really have it tough. For the guy you kinda like and would like to spend more of your time with, what do you do? I mean you really like him and would like to get a Blizzard together this Friday night, but that doesn't mean you want his tongue down your throat, right? And he might think that when you accept his invitation to a date that you are accepting the tongue, too. Guys speak a different language, you know?

Then there is the other guy who you don't care to be around at all but you don't (or at least shouldn't) want to demolish him by telling him that he makes your skin crawl. If you love God and care about those He made, then you will even treat the guys that give you the creeps with respect. You still want to demonstrate what is best for him as he finds his way in life. And you can be a big part of that by being an example to him on how to treat people like a unique creation of God.

There is probably a third group, but maybe not a lot of guys fit in that category. They are OK to be around, I mean they don't gross you out or anything but you wouldn't want to date them. They are funny or interesting in their own way but no hint of romantic feelings are there. How do you treat them? What does that relationship look like, especially since you may not want them to get the wrong idea about what that relationship means. You aren't saying that you like him as your date for Friday night, but you aren't thinking, "I'm going to vomit!"

Of course, if the answers to any of these scenarios could be answered by seven simple rules, life would be easier for everyone. As you have seen already, my gal Heather has avoided the laws, or do's and don'ts. And she has done this simply because you and your friends are completely unique. No one was ever created just like you and no one ever will be. So I would love to give you exactly what to do and say in every situation but that would probably only work 5 percent of the time (on a good day).

So where do we go from here? Well, in football they showed us that little line at the end of the field and called it the goal line. And since I was smaller than nearly everyone else on the field, I learned to avoid people hitting me by running as fast as I could toward the goal. So here is how to avoid some hits yourself . . . the goal is *love.*

Hmmm . . . I can tell by the squint in your forehead that my answer isn't exactly what you wanted. Stay with me because showing love to people not only helps them in the long run, but it actually benefits you as well. When you understand what real love for others truly is, it opens the door for God to do things in your life that you never imagined possible. Living in a way that shows your love for God not only prevents your heart from being torn apart at the seams but it also provides the opportunity to see Him take the desires of your heart and bring them into reality.

Part of the problem in getting what I'm saying involves what I mean by loving someone. Our world only tells us that you know when you are in love because you feel really tingly inside when you are around that person. Romantic love comes and goes with our emotions depending on how you feel from day to day. A passionate kiss and a huge bouquet of red roses attached to a bag of Skittles does make you "feel" love. The problem with that "love" is that when the Skittles are gone and the flowers are wilted, *it* also wilts. The love that God wants us to show to others, which is a mirror image of the way He loves us, is much different.

I like to say that love is looking out for the interests of others when they haven't yet realized the best way to look out for themselves. If someone's going to drink poison because they are having a bad day, you would wrestle the poison out of their hands whether they wanted you to or not. That would be the loving thing to do. Or how about if your best friend is cutting herself with a razor blade but she tells you not to tell anyone? Would it be a loving thing to do to allow her to continue hurting herself if you really cared about her?

Well, these illustrations are a little easier to grasp because they involve physical harm. You can see a cut on someone's arm but you can't see one on his or her heart. The difficulty comes when we start having to make decisions about areas that will hurt them emotionally or spiritually, or both. Many times guys and girls who already have wounded hearts seek to cover the pain with ways that create more pain. I was that way. And I thought I was healing that wound rather than making it deeper. I fooled myself into thinking that doing something that felt right to cover my pain was actually love. None of us want to participate in the slashing of a person's soul but that was what I did and unfortunately many of us do.

I remember a girl in high school who sat behind me in geography. She was pretty and even popular. Unfortunately, she was popular for the wrong reason. She tried desperately to get my attention by gently blowing on the back of my neck and even tickling me with her long fingernails. For someone I hardly know to use the opportunity of where I was sitting to get some attention only made me lose respect for her. She desperately needed a guy's attention and would do most anything to get it. She was hurting herself by "selling out" and paying whatever price necessary to feel special. She was worth more than that. She was worth waiting for a guy to win her properly at the right time in her life. Many guys didn't do the loving thing by saying, "No thanks." Most took advantage of her. She needed someone to look out for her best interest when she wasn't able to look out for her own.

Looking out for others' best interests can be tough. (I can promise you though, it will also save you a ton of disappointment. Trust me—been there, done that.) But how do we do it? That is the question. Well Paul did a great job of laying down some timeless principles that you can use to guide your decisions, both in what you say and in what you do. Look at his teaching to a group of people who needed to hear how to treat each other: "Love cares more for others than for self . . . isn't always 'me first,' . . . takes pleasure in the flowering of truth" (1 Cor. 13:4-6). In other words: Love is showing someone you genuinely care about them and their well being.

Paul gives us this idea that love continues to look out for someone else even if they don't make you feel good or even if they hurt you. It also shows us that doing the wrong thing out of a desire to make someone feel loved is also not a good idea.

If you really care about the guys you are around, then you will not want to say, wear, or do anything that could hurt them physically, emotionally, or spiritually. If he is allowed to see you naked before marriage then you have wounded his soul and his heart even though his emotions enjoy it at the time. Even tempting a guy you are dating to push the relationship physically by not holding to your agreed upon boundaries will cause him and you pain. We can't see the wound like a physical one but it is there in our souls.

To be honest very few guys are spiritually mature enough not to push. Most of us guys haven't been taught very well how to truly love a girl. We are just selfish and want to feel good. Several indicators can tell you if a guy knows truly how to love. For instance, if any guy is really acting loving toward you, he won't be jealous of you for just talking with another guy. He also would never insist that you do something you don't feel comfortable doing in order to prove your love. That would mean if he starts to push the limits, that you would show him love even if it means ending the relationship with him. That may be very difficult to do, especially if you are attracted to him. But you won't be loving him by giving in to his wrong advances because sin brings death . . . death to your friendship and hopes for each other.

Getting to the goal line of love is a journey of peril and danger. Like a running back being handed the ball with eleven other guys trying to crush him, you are trying to navigate through a maze of many potential knock-downs. Learning to sidestep them and keep headed toward the goal is difficult. I know when I was a teenager I tripped over the obstacle of "feel good now." Whatever pain I was feeling could be salved by a sloppy kiss with my gal H. However, I realized too late that I wasn't loving Heather, I was really ripping a deeper wound open in both of us because my actions were selfishly motivated. True love doesn't seek its own. I'm sorry, Heather.

Let's look again at those three groups and try to get some principles or guidelines and boil all this down a bit into something bite-size.

After Each Other

That special guy that you think about often is the one that has the most potential for a good relationship *and* the potential for the biggest disaster. It is good to think about him like a best friend. As you share your thoughts, dreams, and opinions with one another you can find out who he really is. Enjoy him, but also realize that if he feels the same way about you, there is a magnet pulling you together. The stronger the attraction, the more potential for hurt exists. He will probably try to cross the line of what is acceptable. It may be helpful to talk with your youth group or youth leader about some suggestions of where to draw the line if you're not sure. Generally "what everyone else is doing" is not the best goal to shoot for. *You must be able to let him go if you see he hasn't learned how to love unselfishly yet! You can't fix him and the only way to help him is to break off the relationship.* Remember, you are worth waiting for—that special someone must earn you with unselfish love!

Guys After You

Guys who are attracted to you but you aren't really interested in can be a temptation to play with, but be kind. If you are a little insecure in yourself you may be tempted to flirt a little bit just to get a thrill when you see them light up. But since love never seeks its own fulfillment at another's expense, you wouldn't be able to get God's blessing by doing that kind of thing. It's not loving to play with a guy's hormones or his heart. It is tempting to use someone's attraction toward you as a toy, especially if it gets you points with your circle of friends who just want to see someone get dashed to pieces. Be honest with him though. Tell him he is a nice guy and point out one of his good qualities but tell him that for right now the two of you wouldn't be a good match.

Guys for the Hereafter

Those guys who you aren't really drawn to but you aren't repelled by are the best place for you to learn, observe, and get accustomed to guys. We are a little like an alien species at first. But the longer you are around us you can become better at spotting which of us are trouble and which ones are capable of a healthy relationship. Guys who aren't after you and whom you feel at ease being around can be a great source of companionship. Remember again, act in love! Flirting with even the touch of your hand can ruin a good friendship. Don't send mixed signals. Be honest. Tell him you just want to learn how guys think—for real—so that you can have good friendships with them.

There is a tension between what a guy is after to fill his physical needs and what a girl will do in order to fill her emotional needs. His desire to feel good physically and a girl's need to feel special can both be filled in the wrong way bringing disaster to both. The wrong way to go about that is so tempting and seems so right. Both of the needs are legitimate and were put there by God but our enemy wants us to try to meet them in the wrong way. The wrong path only leads to heartache, emptiness, and tears. Paul really wants us to love by taking pleasure in truth. And the truth is that compromising what is right in order to keep a guy or make him or yourself feel good isn't love. So, just be loving to guys in your life, especially in the way you dress, the way you talk, and the way you touch.

WRAP UP

Are you an Olympics nut like I am?

They hook me every time. My B even went out and bought a satellite dish where we were in Africa a week before the games began. He knew I couldn't miss them. Since it is no small joke to get a satellite dish in Kenya, he hurried and hurried and somehow managed to get it hooked up and running a day before the opening ceremony! Ah, my hero!

There is something about the Olympics that brings out the best in the athletes and makes it a scream to watch. They try harder. They give more. They aim higher than they ever did before. The Olympics give us so many stories that make us gasp, hope, and cry.

I remember one of my favorite stories happened probably when you were still running around outside with a sucker in your mouth and begging your big sister to push you on the swing. I, however, was glued to the tube. And, by the way, it was a well-worth-it glue.

It was women's gymnastics team finals night. The title of it always makes me chuckle, seeing as most of these "women" look like they're ten years old and weigh about fifty pounds! Did they ever think of changing it to "girls'" gymnastics or something?

I had no idea that the competition was going to be so close, though. Of course I had hoped that America would win . . . duh! But since they had never won before as a team in gymnastics, I wasn't totally certain that they would pull it off this time. After all, their competition was pretty deep: Russia, Romania, and China.

The scores were close when it came time for the very last apparatus. Russia, who was in second place, was scheduled to finish up on the floor routine. America, who was holding on to a tight lead (go States!), was finishing up on the vault.

Everything looked like it was going pretty okay for Team USA until their second-to-last member fell twice on her vaults. Now in girls' gymnastics—um, excuse me—I mean in "women's" gymnastics, as you might know, each team member competing gets two attempts on the vault. Then they add the teammates' top scores up together but they get to drop the lowest one.

Since the second-to-last girl had fallen twice, her score would have to be the one that was dropped. Obviously. And if America was going to walk away wearing her first-ever gymnastics team gold medal for the gals, it would need to be got by the last girl scheduled to run.

Her name was Kerri.

Kerri Strug.

Now, according to the coaches, Kerri might not have been their pick for someone to stand into such a huge spot. She had always been considered the "baby" of the group. The coaches even used softer words with her when correcting her because they said she just wasn't all that tough. But, regardless of all of that, the schedule had already been made.

Kerri was up.

The weight of a nation rested heavily on her eighty-eight-pound frame. The memory of her teammate falling before her tumbled around in her brain. Would she do the same?

Only time could tell.

Kerri saluted the judges.

She ran.

She vaulted.

And like her teammate before her . . . yep, she also fell.

Instead of Kerri's first attempt giving her and her teammates the gold medal, it gave her a sprained ankle and torn ligaments to boot. She stood back up after her fall and felt the pain pierce beyond mere tissue and plunge deeper into her soul.

How could she try again?

She could barely even walk.

On the sidelines, Kerri heard the urgings of her teammates. She knew the years of sacrifice and practice they had all put in together. She had felt their friendships. This particular team was a team of unprecedented bonding. She felt their hopes resting in her. She felt her own hopes as well.

With these hopes lifting her a bit, Kerri somehow managed to stumble back to the starting point. The voice of her coach followed her, "You can do it, Kerri," he shouted. "You can do it!"

Could she?

She didn't know.

But, at the very least, she would certainly give it another go.

Her salute went up for the judges. Kerri gazed down the path. She took a deep breath. Then she ran. She vaulted. And she landed.

Score!

Barely able to hold her foot down through the pain, Kerri hobbled and saluted once again, long enough for the judges to assess her. Then she collapsed on the mat in tears, exhaustion, and relief.

She had done it. She had done what she needed to do. And she had done it well.

Kerri's points went up. They were good enough for the gold!

I cheered!

I shouted!

I bawled!

After all, how often do we get to see someone go again after such an obvious fall? How often do we get to see someone set her own pain aside and give it another try for the benefit of the ultimate goal?

How often do we feel the power of a team and hear the confidence of a coach shouting words of belief?

Not that often, at least I don't think.

And, sorry to say, that's way, yes, totally way too bad.

Because we're all a little bit like Kerri sometimes. Life and its struggles have left us limping, doubting, or down. Maybe we've tripped ourselves up through destructive or rash choices. Or maybe other people have tripped us up by playing us or hurting us somehow. It can happen. And it does. Most of us have been played. Don't think you're the only one.

It doesn't matter, though, so much how the tripping came about. What matters is what we decide to do now. Sure, we're down and we've been hurt. Maybe we didn't really trust the rules that were given to us and we're soaking in the consequences of that now. Or maybe we tried to dress like a pop-star diva and we've earned the rep of cheap chow. We know there's still another run to take on this path called life but wouldn't it be easier to just skip it? Sell out. Blend back into the crowd. Who wants to risk another disappointment? Who wants to risk letting ourselves or other people down? After all, who's to say we could even make it . . . that we could even pull the whole thing off well?

So we stand there. Debating.

Do we dare go again? And if so, how?

Before you decide, let me tell you a little something more about Kerri's time that I purposefully left out of her story before. In an interview later on after her gold medal, the reporter asked Kerri how she had managed to do what she had done.

Kerri said, "I kept thinking with each step, it [the pain] would go away, but it didn't . . . I kept saying, 'There's something wrong with me.' . . . So I said a little prayer: Please, Lord, help me out here."[1]

See, Kerri knew that there was something wrong, sure. She wasn't making it up. But rather than give up or pretend that there wasn't anything wrong at all and try to go it alone, she remembered God. She remembered that she wasn't on her own.

"I said a little prayer: Please, Lord, help me out here."

Hey you, girlfriend of mine, have you ever felt like something's wrong? Like everyone else is the normal one? Have you ever felt like Kerri, that with "each step, it [the pain] would go away, but it didn't." And so you started thinking that "there's something wrong with me."

You've got a limp or a sprain or a ligament out of place?

Want in on a secret?

So do I.

We all do.

Otherwise we wouldn't be trying so hard to cover it.

We wouldn't be bending the rules in an effort to set our own. We wouldn't be dressing the chameleon with whatever is current or in. We wouldn't be surrounding ourselves so easily with just anyone breathing and calling them friends so we don't have to feel alone. We wouldn't be longing for that guy who we know must complete us. We wouldn't forget, like we so often do, that we're really not out here on our own.

Yep, life is tricky. 'Tis true. And it's tough. Maybe we've made some really awful choices before. But do you want to know the good thing? The game's not over. And we don't have to go it alone.

"I said a little prayer: Please, Lord, help me out here."

Do something for me—do something for you. Pray, "Please, Lord, help me out here," because He's dying to answer you.

And if you listen really closely, you can hear the sound of His voice. He's cheering you on. It's your turn to dazzle. Can you hear Him, "You can do it! You can do it! Go girl! Go now!"

Kerri went and got the gold. She got it because she tried and she tried and she tried the way she should. She could have given up, but she didn't. She could have just collapsed on the mat after her stumble. Few could have blamed her, not after her fall. But, instead, she got up, she prayed, and she took another go at her turn on the vault. And thanks to the cheers of those around her, thanks to her coach, and thanks to God, Kerri has a bit of gold hanging around her now and forevermore.

So what do you say?

Life's been confusing at times?

Got a few bruises. Got a few scars. A few doubts. Heard a few lies.

How about standing back up and starting all over. Because in this game, you get another try.

You can do it. You can gaze down the path. You can run, leap, and fly.

I'll see you on the podium. You'll be the one with the golden gleam in your eyes.

GO **GIRL!**

STUDY GUIDE

PART 1: RULES

1. Heather writes that "rules show themselves as a threat to our power." Why is it that many teenagers struggle to obey rules? What rules in your life do you wish you could abolish or change?

2. Do you find that your friends encourage you to keep rules or break them?

3. Henry was thankful for the rule of driving under 55 miles per hour. It's a rule that may have saved his life. What rules in your life are you thankful for?

4. Heather took pride in the rule not to get drunk or swear. What rules do you keep that you take pride in?

5. Why do we sometimes think that keeping rules earns us more of God's love?

6. Why do we find it so difficult to trust God, our parents, and others and end up questioning authority?

7. If Jesus knew we would fail Him, why did He allow Himself to be crucified? What does that tell you about His love for you?

8. In Africa, the sound of a rooster crowing reminds Heather of God's love for her. What helps you remember how much God loves you?

9. Explain how you can feel free by staying inside the guidelines of rules.

10. How does love free us to follow rules? What rules have you followed because of love?

PART 2: RAGS

1. When have you looked at how someone was dressed and made a judgment about them that was wrong?

2. In Kenya, wearing shorts and showing the knees is very inappropriate . . . a no-no. What is a no-no in our culture?

3. What do you want to communicate to others by the way you dress?

4. How can a girl dress to tease? Why does Henry coach girls to not do that? How can you dress to "leave some mystery in the air"?

5. What impact does it have on a guy when he can see a girl's underwear peeking out of her jeans? How can you help?

6. Why do you think God made guys so visual?

7. How does the autonomic nervous system (ANS) help you understand guys more?

8. Henry writes that "being kind in the way you dress is love." How is that true?

9. How does "dressing with humility" mean letting go of the need to impress? Why do many girls feel the need to impress others by the way they dress?

10. The challenge is for a girl to be clothed in mystery, clothed in love, and wrapped in rags reflecting her worth from above. What does the Bible say about your worth?

PART 3: RELATIONSHIPS

1. God made us for relationships. We can't go it alone. What do you look for in relationships with other girls?

2. How do true friendships make us "stronger, snappier, and smarter in a world full of zips and bumbles"?

3. What makes Jesus your best friend?

4. Let's have some fun! Who are the following girls in your life:

   a. Go-To Girl—someone you can go to when things get tough.
   b. Go-Go Girl—someone who makes you giggle.
   c. Go-Through-It Girl—the loyal relationship, someone who will stick by you.

5. How can you identify and avoid the "Go-Without Girls"?

6. Look at the list. What kind of girl are you?

7. Look at the list of guys to avoid. How can your friends help you stay clear of these guys?

8. Of the guys to avoid, which one is the hardest to identify?

9. Think for a second about your future husband. Describe him.

10. Read Galatians 5:22–23. Why is a guy who exhibits these qualities worth waiting for?

ENDNOTES

MOCHA MEMORIES

1. S. K. Henshaw, *U.S. teenage pregnancy statistics with comparative statistics for women aged 20–24* (New York: The Alan Guttmacher Institute, 2004).

CHAPTER 2: IT'S ALL ABOUT TRUST

1. Joshua Harris, *Not Even a Hint: Guarding Your Heart Against Lust* (Sisters, OR: Multnomah, 2003), 17.
2. John Piper, *A Godward Life, Book II* (Sisters, OR.: Multnomah, 1999), 227.

CHAPTER 3: IT'S ALL ABOUT THE RULER

1. Natalie Moe, *Ignite the Fire* (Grand Rapids: Kregel, 2000).

CHAPTER 4: THE RULEBOOK

1. Max Lucado, *A Love Worth Giving* (Nashville: W, 2002), 10.

CHAPTER 6: IT'S ALL ABOUT ANS

1. Donald Trump interview, http://www.askmen.com/ women/models_200/230_melania_knauss.html.
2. Michael Ventre, MSNBC.com, August 5, 2003.
3. Rashod D. Ollison, "Thighs and Whimpers: Timberlake and Aguilera Need to Get Real and Drop the Silly Disguises," *Baltimore Sun*, August 17, 2003.

CHAPTER 8: **TRADING THEM IN**

1. Britney Spears interview, "Britney Spears Celebrity Stature Continues to Climb," *Newsweek,* November 3, 2003.

CHAPTER 10: **BEING CHOOSY**

1. *Amadeus: Director's Cut* DVD, "Making of Amadeus" special feature, 2001.

CHAPTER 11: **ROLE CALL!**

1. Cecilia M. Vega and Jeremy Hay, "Plane takes off from Two Rock ranch without pilot," *Santa Rosa* (Santa Rosa, CA) *Press Democrat,* December 27, 2001.

WRAP UP

1. E. M. Swift, "Profile in Courage," *Sports Illustrated*, August 5, 1996, http://sportsillustrated.cnn.com/events/1996/olympics/weekly/960805/gymnastics.html.

IGNITE THE FIRE

"Practical . . . and refreshing . . . I needed to read this book just like any person out there looking for truth."

—Kevin Max, recording artist

Is Jesus relevant today? Is He the answer?

A former international model uses her experiences with God to show that God does make a difference. Using her own journey to illustrate, author Natalie Moe ignites a hope and passion found only in reliance on God. Full of relevant questions and applicable Scripture verses, this book points teens to the truth.

0-8254-3342-8 • 160 pages

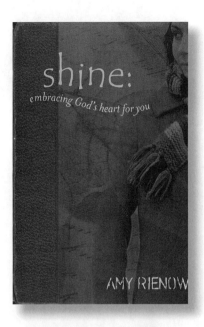

SHINE

EMBRACING GOD'S HEART FOR YOU

"God created you to shine. Do you believe it?"

Most young women who've spent any time in the church know the fundamental truths. They know who they are in Christ, and that they should find their identity in Him rather than beauty, popularity, or boys. Written for the young woman who has learned all the correct answers in church but says, "so what?" this book shows her how to live out the truth she's always known.

0-8254-3580-3 • 160 pages